Gillan Vase

Through Love to Life

A Novel. Vol. 1

Gillan Vase

Through Love to Life
A Novel. Vol. 1

ISBN/EAN: 9783744759885

Printed in Europe, USA, Canada, Australia, Japan

Cover: Foto ©Thomas Meinert / pixelio.de

More available books at **www.hansebooks.com**

BY

GILLAN VASE

A novel is a subjective epopee, wherein the author begs permission to treat the world after his fashion: the question therefore is, has he a fashion? the rest will attend to itself—GOETHE

IN THREE VOLUMES

VOL. I.

LONDON

SMITH, ELDER, & CO., 15 WATERLOO PLACE

1889

CONTENTS

OF

THE FIRST VOLUME.

———◦◦◦———

THROUGH LOVE TO LIFE.

CHAPTER I.

ROWS.

I spell my name with the Y.—ESMOND.

It was a quarter to seven when the row began
—just before dinner-time.

Notice that I say *the* row. A row was as
common in our house as—say, in Ireland, or
in the Chamber of Deputies in France. A
row wouldn't have been worth recording.

But this row taught me two or three things,
which I never afterwards forgot.

Is it not something for a man to learn—a
man *in futuro*, for I had been but recently

breeched—that woman is as *False* as she is *Fair?* and that fathers and mothers may be?— well, never mind what!

I was in the hall. Let me confess the truth. I had been robbing my parents of sundry pears and sundry bunches of grapes, and conscience had driven me into a recess behind a naked and extremely chubby boy in white marble, who was always aiming at every one who passed him with a bow and arrow. Down behind him I crouched, waiting for an opportunity to escape.

I was rather interested in this boy, for mamma's friends used to say that I was very like him (when mamma was there), and used to poke their fingers in my cheeks and pull my curls, and call me 'a little love,' and ask me how many *I* meant to shoot when I began.

I wondered how many *he* shot. I never saw him hit anybody myself, but Thérèse,

mamma's French maid, said he did sometimes.
And she was all dimples and white teeth when
I asked her, and sobbing before she had
answered, her pretty hand upon her bosom as
if a sudden pain had sprung up there and was
more than she could bear.

'Did he ever hit you, Thérèse?' I asked.

'Hit me? Oh, but he is foolish, the little
one! He is always hitting me, my little
monsieur.'

'When, Thérèse?'

'All the days, *petit*. When men smile at
me, and they do *sometimes*, why I—I feel a
pain here, and that is his arrow.'

She was showing all her pearls again.

'Does he hit you when I put my arms
round your neck and tell you that I love you
better than anyone in the world?—no, not
better than my nurse,' I added, with a great
feeling of compunction.

'See how he knows already how to make

love, the little one,' laughed Thérèse.   'Wait till you are a man, *mon enfant*, and break hearts then.'

'Is it good to break hearts?   Papa whips me sometimes when I break other things.'

'Good?   I do not know.   It is very easy and *bien drôle*; funny, you call it; and it makes you laugh, and the other cry.   That is why I laugh and cry and sing and dance : Tra, la, la, la, la.   *L'amour*—But what can a *bébé* like you know about love?'

Very little, I dare say.   But as she laughed, I felt a sharp, sharp pain in the spot where my heart went pit-a-pat, keen as an arrow. I looked up in sudden passion to the marble image, still levelling his bow — yet with a difference.   Some effect of falling light or shade had changed his arch smile into a cruel sneer.

Having introduced you to Thérèse, let me go back to the row.

From my hiding-place I had a good view
of the staircase, and could also see every door
leading into the hall. To my right was my
father's room, the oaken door hidden behind
another covered with baize which swung to
and fro on noiseless hinges. Beyond that was
the dining-room, its door slightly ajar, as I
had left it when I had fled before William and
the butler with my booty. For I had been
tempted down into these lower regions as our
first mother was tempted—by lust after
forbidden fruit.

I was looking earnestly into this room in
order to take advantage of the first opportunity for escape. The butler's calm face was
discomposed; he had found out the disarrange-
ment of his dishes, and was, no doubt, inwardly
swearing revenge. I watched him repair the
breaches I had made, noiselessly putting the
master-touch to the *tout ensemble*, while William
stood at his side, possibly profiting from the

lesson he was receiving, but with a far-away
look in his honest blue eyes and a pallor over
his usually ruddy cheek, hardly like the
visible and outward signs of inward satisfaction.

'The de'il tak' him,' muttered the butler,
who was a Scotchman; 'my finest pears and
juiciest bunch of grapes!'

Of course. Did he think I'd risk my
reputation for nothing?

'Cruel and heartless,' murmured William,
' and yet so pretty, so pretty.'

I was a pretty boy—I had been told that
many and many a time (by mamma's friends
principally)—but *cruel* and *heartless*! O'ho,
William, look out for nips!'

And then they turned together and my
opportunity was come.

But no! a footfall on the stairs. A sweet
saucy face appearing above the banister. I
slunk back again into my corner. I couldn't

trust Thérèse. She might connive at my escape or might betray me, just according to her humour.

Her humour was dangerous now. Her eyelids were reddened, and in the centre of each pale cheek burned a crimson spot; yet out of her brown eyes flashed a light so intense that the staircase seemed illuminated with it, and her mouth was wreathed with dimples. Somebody had angered Thérèse, and somebody was going to get punished for it.

She came down the broad oaken steps slowly; her shapely little head erect and haughty, her smiling lips quivering a little. As she passed the statue behind which I was crouching, she turned her sparkling eyes full upon it, clenched her little fist, and laughed. Then more quickly, and with an air of passionate resolution, she passed on to my father's room, pulled open the baize-covered door, and rapped sharply upon the oaken one behind it—once, twice.

My father himself appeared in answer to the summons.

As she raised her beautiful, agitated face to his red, pompous, overbearing one, I felt rather than saw that a second spectator had appeared upon the scene. A second heart began to beat in quick unison with mine.

'What is it?' said my father.

'It is madame who has bidden me to go,' answered the girl, sobbing. 'It is madame who has raised the foot to kick me out of the house. Is it that I am a slave to lick the dust at madame's bidding? I am come to say my adieux to monsieur. *Je m'en vais.*'

'No, you don't,' said my father.

'I am sensible of the kindness of monsieur,' continued Thérèse; 'I have a heart—I. And then *le petit* will cry after me. But I have

my honour too, and " slut " and " hussy " are
words that stick like pitch and burn like fire.
Je m'en vais.'

As she uttered these words for the second
time, the shadow of a sound fell over my ears
and deafened them. Was it Eros himself
crying out in tones of smothered agony,
' Thérèse! Thérèse! Mamsell Thérèse ! ' ?

I saw my father's arm around her waist,
and her face raised to his with a maddening
look upon it—a look full of simulated coyness
and sly invitation, and then——

And then the grapes in my hand turned
sour as vinegar, and the pears in my trouser-
pockets heavy as lead.

The row was at its fiercest when I became
conscious of it. There was a rustle of silken
skirts, a stamping of heavy feet, hoarse
threatenings, and through all, the sharp sound
of a woman's voice, envenomed with bitter
sarcasm and biting innuendo. It ended with

the usual wind-up of hysterics, during which my mother was carried away prostrate.

Yet, though she fasted and my father dined, the victory was hers, and I knew it as well as anyone.

I was no longer afraid of discovery. Pain had driven out fear. I walked boldly into the dining-room, and sitting down in a corner half hidden by a heavy silken curtain, watched my father dine. The butler watched him too, and so did William.

He didn't seem to enjoy his dinner much, I thought. He took it, as I took medicine, in great gulps, washing all down with copious draughts of wine. Once he broke out into a furious passion, dashing a full wineglass on to the table, and staining the white damask deep red with its contents.

The dinner was over at last. It seemed a long time before the butler and William went away, but they went finally. And then he gave up trying to seem not to care. He leaned his head upon his hand, so that I could see the silver threads running through his hair, and groaned and struck the table with his fist until all the crystal on it trembled.

I had been feeling towards him like a judge towards a criminal; now my mind suddenly changed its attitude. We were both wrongdoers and both suffering.

'Papa,' I said, 'papa!'

He looked up with a start; then his blood-shot eye brightened, the heavy frown passed away from his forehead, and his lips parted to a smile.

'Hoighty-toighty!' he said; 'you there, little mannikin?'

We were both wrongdoers and both suffering, nevertheless I had a burning word to say, and meant to say it. Yet my resolution was faltering fast. He was looking at me with a piteous longing in his eyes—a longing

I knew how to interpret. He was not over-sensitive, but the sharp, bitter words of his wife might have wounded a tougher-skinned nature even than his, and he was bleeding inwardly. He wanted a morsel of the only cure for heart wounds. He was hungering for a fragment of love.

Yet I hung back still, even though he put out both red, hard, beringed hands, and would fain have drawn me to his knee.

'Have a drop of wine, my boy?'

Child-like, I abandoned the weapon I held to grasp the one he offered. I cried out in a passion, born of the conflict within me.

'It is wine makes you so red and ugly, and I hate it.'

He half rose and clenched his fist. I drew back, involuntarily ducking my head to avoid the blow I expected.

But he only laughed, repeating my words as if they had been a joke.

' Makes me red and ugly, does it? Very well, you sha'n't have wine if you don't like it. You shall have some figs. Ring the bell and bid the lazy brutes bring you some figs.'

' I don't want anything to eat, papa. I only want to tell you——'

' Well?'

' That——'

' Well?'

' That——' And in spite of all my efforts I burst out a-crying.

' Good gracious, what's the matter? Tell me what it is, my boy. Everything I have is yours. I've been working all my life that you may have everything you want.'

' But I want——'

' Speak out, don't be afraid.'

A certain sense of childish dignity came now to my aid. I wiped my eyes, drew up my head, straightened my back, and spoke out like a man.

'I want Thérèse. I love her. I shall be a man some day, and I am going to marry her.'

If I had sprung up suddenly into a man before his eyes, he could not have looked more confounded. Then the humour of the thing struck him. He burst into a loud fit of laughter, and laughed until the tears ran down his cheeks.

'You are beginning early, young man.'

I resented his ridicule almost as much as I had resented the foregoing insult. There was no danger of my crying now. My heart was swelling high, but it was with pride and indignation. My body seemed to swell with it.

'And I don't want—I don't *choose*,' I added haughtily, 'that anyone shall kiss her but me. William is only a servant. *You* have got mamma, and ought to be content.'

My argument was simple and childlike enough. But it led him back into the old track, wherein his soul had been wandering so drearily. He seemed to forget—he might well forget—that he was speaking to a child.

'Yes,' he repeated, 'I've got mamma, and I ought to be content. And she's no French adventuress, come from nowhere, and owned by nobody, but a baronet's daughter, and I ought to be more than content. And she leads me the life of a—a baronet's daughter's husband, and I ought to be most content. So I am! So I am!'

But he looked like a wild and furious animal as he got up and paced the room, and he looked like an animal bruising its head against the bars of its cage, when he brought his fist again into thundering contact with the mahogany.

'I was once an adventurer myself,' he continued, 'and might have been a different man if she—I mean, I might have remained one of a beggarly lot. But now I'm Charles Smythe, Esquire—with the Y, remember! And they

know me well on 'Change. And I could buy
up hundreds of pauper baronets and bankrupt
lords. And I'm a greater man than I ever
hoped to be. And I ought to be content.
Good God! so I am!'

He had forgotten that I was there until
he caught sight of me, pale and terror-
stricken.

'Go back to your nurse,' he cried, like a
man beside himself, 'and learn from her to
be a better man than your father.'

CHAPTER II.

MY FIRST LOVE.

Aber die Natur behauptet mit Nachdruck ihre Rechte, und da sie niemals willkürlich fordert, so nimmt sie, unbefriedigt, auch keine Forderung zurück.

SCHILLER (Anmuth und Würde).

NOTWITHSTANDING my opposition, and notwithstanding my father's, Thérèse had to go the next day, and, to add to my bewilderment and dismay and despair, William went with her.

There had been a deep, deep reason for that indignant clause in my reproach to my father: 'William is only a servant'—a reason so profound that my childish brain only just perceived, and had not yet grasped and defined, it. Surely *he* could not be my rival

—he, the only man in the house who ever found fault with Thérèse, the only one who never told her how light her step was, nor how glossy her wavy hair, nor how bright were her dark eyes, nor how round and smooth her neck, nor how enchanting her dimples. Other men said these things, for the saying of which I cordially hated them (I felt, but could not express), and only William never did.

Yet a secret instinct showed me that his blame meant more than their praise, his pained look of disapproval more than their flattery. Sometimes, behind her back, these sycophants would laugh at Thérèse, calling her a spoiled chit, a minx, a heartless French coquette, and the like, while William would keep indignant silence or break out into indignant defence, always saying that she was a deal better—a thousand times better—than she would appear.

And once I was witness to a scene between these two which tended to make my fleeting impression into a permanent, yet still incomprehensible, one.

It was evening, I remember, and my nurse was putting my little sisters to bed, while I was intent on finishing a second Tower of Babel. I was alone in the day nursery, laying my bricks to the time of a tune my nurse was humming in the room adjoining, and wondering as I built which voice was the sweeter—hers or Thérèse's, and which of the two I really loved the best.

Thinking of Thérèse, I began to fancy I could hear her light step on the landing outside, a heavier one following it. I put down the brick in my hand and listened intently; and now I distinctly heard a low, sweet, mocking laugh and a scuffle; then a cry of anger.

I ran to the door, opened it and looked out.

I knew it was Thérèse, yet it was not William whom I had expected to see beside her, nor had I ever fancied *him* with his arm around her waist and his hand close to her crimson cheek.

'Has he been beating you, Thérèse?' I asked.

She was laughing, showing all her white teeth and dimples as she pushed him from her, yet for all that she was in a furious passion, her eyes flashing and her bodice rising and falling like the waves of an angry sea.

'Has he been beating you?' I repeated in my wisdom and knowledge of human nature, and I ran to stroke her red cheek and lay my own against it.

'Yes, he has, he has!' she cried violently, pushing me from her, striking the air with her outstretched hands, and all in a tremble from head to foot. 'He has no right to do it.

I'm not a nun to be shut up in a convent. I'm not eighty yet, to have done with life and be ready to die. I'm only a girl, and I want pleasure and sweetness and freedom. I will have what I want. I will, I will!'

It was odd to see how rapidly her speech passed on into action, and how emphatic the action made her words. When she spoke of not being a nun, she drew her white apron over her head and across her dimpled chin, making you scorn the absurd idea with herself. When comparing her own blooming youth to eighty, she wrinkled her smooth forehead, humped her straight back, and drew in her full red lips, shocking you almost as much as if the simulated change had been real. When she had declared that she would have enjoyment and sweetness and liberty, she had raised her longing eyes and parted her coral lips as if about to taste heavenly nectar. With that bright flush upon her usually pale cheek

she had looked then like a female Dionysus—
goddess of pleasure and the lust of it.

I turned angrily towards William. How
could I know, child that I was, whether she
were claiming a divine right or stretching forth
impious hands to clutch a gift from the altar?
I only knew that she was beautiful, that her
beauty made my heart ache, and every fibre
in me vibrate, and that I loved her.

I turned towards William and saw in his
face the same feeling animating mine, only
intensified. For while in me it was as child-
like as my body, in him it was in the full
strength of its manhood.

'Thérèse, Thérèse!' he cried; 'Mamsell
Thérèse!'

I faltered. I still propounded the foolish
question upon my lips, but I did so now fully
conscious that the answer would be beyond me.

'Why did you beat Thérèse?' I asked.
'How dared you beat her?'

Before he could answer, a gentle but firm summons to my nursery forced me to give up the riddle or find an answer to it myself. But before leaving the two I saw a sight which so complicated it that I was forced to abandon the idea of a solution in despair.

I saw that incomprehensible Thérèse, who had been twisting the corner of her white apron into a hard knot and mercilessly lashing her pretty fingers with the same, suddenly dart forward, throw herself upon her knees before the footman, and, taking his hard hand, press it to her lips. Then she vanished down the staircase, leaving William still standing there, like a huge image carved in stone.

Heighho! There are things in this world hard to understand!

. . . . .

It was the day after the row that William and Thérèse came together into my nursery to say good-bye to me and to my nurse.

Oh, that nursery, wherein much bread was cast upon the waters, many good seeds sown, which seemed long lost among the tares, but which, I humbly hope, eventually bore some good fruit—I can fancy myself there again, high up among the chimneypots, and see again its one smoke-stained window looking out upon them, its one solitary unframed print representing the rich man feasting with his boon companions and sick Lazarus at his gates, its one worn leather-covered easy-chair, wherein sat the house's guardian angel—the one righteous being, I have since thought, who saved us from destruction !

For the weather outside in the dark heart of the City of London was not more unpleasantly variable than was the weather within.   Inside too there was the change from storm to apathetic calm, from darkness unrelieved to darkness visible, from falling rain to fog impenetrable.   Two things we never had—the bow of Hope and the sunshine; or rather only in that one warm heart, where they were no flitting lodgers but perpetual inmates.

It was a wild and stormy day in late autumn when Thérèse went away. A fierce, dry wind was raging through the City, making the windows rattle again and bringing clouds of dust against our house. Inside there had been a fresh row, and some of its angry breath had risen up to us. Even my nurse sighed a little as she sat rocking the baby in the cradle, and her mouth twitched at the corners as it did when she was grieved.

They came in together side by side, William and Thérèse, and even I was struck by the contrast they presented, the girl's beauty seeming more delicate and lovely than ever compared with the man's strong, square sturdiness, her petulancy painfully in dissonance with his great gentleness. I remember his wanting to relieve her of some trifle, and the sharp way in which she declined his help, as clearly as if it happened yesterday.

Thérèse was in a dozen different moods as usual, and it was impossible to say which mood was the dominant one. She had been crying, for her trim bodice still rose and fell convulsively, yet she was laughing too as merrily as if grief were the best joke in the world. She had just spoken so sharply to William that the tears had sprung into my nurse's eyes, and now she looked up into his face and touched his arm in a manner which made the simple action like a passionate caress.

'I am come to say my adieux,' she said in her rich, soft, full contralto voice. 'Monsieur talks like a man, but madame has gained the victory as ever. Madame will have to paint herself for the future, or get an Englishwoman to do it. *Bon Dieu, une Anglaise !*'

How she managed it heaven knows, but

for a second she stood there transformed before us; her round shoulders squared, her bright eyes half-veiled in ostentatious mock-modesty, her mobile French mouth drawn down at the corners, her smoothly fitting dress creased and angular. Nay, even her hair seemed to participate in the change, and to fall around her graceful head in stiffer curls than usual. In the twinkling of an eye she had become an Englishwoman—the typical Englishwoman of the Parisian stage.

'How funny you look!' said little Florence.

We all laughed—it was impossible to help it. Even William smiled.

'Ah, you do not like your countrywomen, you prefer Thérèse,' said the minx, becoming herself again with a single toss of her saucy head. 'But I must go, and all because of the jealousy of a woman. Now, I am not jealous—*moi*, I never was.'

'You have no need,' said William.

'Who spoke to you, sir?' she returned, flashing round upon him; 'who wants to know what *you* think about it? I never forget but you try to make me remember. I am never happy but you try to make me miserable. I never taste a good thing but you snatch it from my lips. Why was I ever born? Why didn't *le bon Dieu* make me old and hateful and ugly?'

She was sobbing now, her face buried in her hands, her body trembling with the violence of her emotion.

'Hush, hush, my dear!' interposed my nurse gently, rocking the cradle in which slept my youngest sister, little Aileen. 'Those are rough words, and cruel too, when offered in exchange for a great gift—a gift worth every other in the world,' she added, the tears starting to her eyes.

William's ruddy face was pale as death.

and his broad back bent as if there were an unseen load upon it almost insupportable.

'You, you are an angel,' sobbed the girl, falling upon her knees and resting her head upon my nurse's lap. 'You ought to be in heaven, instead of here where it is hell. When I pray to the blessed Mother of God, it is your dear patient face I seem to see, your faithful breast, pierced as hers was. Bless me, bless me before I go.'

'God bless you, my child,' said my nurse, 'and teach you the difference between gold and dross.'

'Amen,' said William.

'As for that,' cried Thérèse, springing to her feet again, 'as for that, there may be two opinions. I've got a ring, old-fashioned and ugly, which is pure gold, and I've got a bracelet—*le voilà!*—only gilded, but I like the bracelet best.'

My nurse was silent ; William turned away
his head to cough.

'*Je préfère bien le bracelet*,' she continued
defiantly, throwing back her loose sleeve and
disclosing an arm which entranced even me,
and at which William gazed as if spellbound.
Regardez ! it is pretty, is it not ?   I think
it is pretty myself—so firm, so soft, so
round, so dimpled.'   She stroked it and
touched it with her lips.   'And the bracelet
looks well upon it.   *Vous trouvez ?*   It isn't
gold, but nobody knows that, and the ring is
ugly, and I can't sell it because it was left me
by my grandmother for good luck.   But I
believe in these '—raising her round arms again
—'much more than in luck.   Therefore I
prefer the bracelet.   *Je le préfère bien.*'

What a cough William had, to be sure,
and how it shook him !

'As for madame,' continued Thérèse, pout-
ing, yet dimpling too, 'she is as foolish as she

is old and ugly. Does she think I would have
let that great, fat, ugly husband of hers kiss
me? Thank heaven, I'm not so hard driven
up for kisses as that! I've no need to go
begging for them. He wanted a kiss—ha !—
and got a *soufflet.*'

'But you did let him kiss you,' I cried, all
my anger reawakened, 'you *did.*'

She laughed, and made as if she would
have kissed me, and laughed louder still when
I drew back in a rage.

'I want you all to myself,' I said ; 'I don't
want to kiss you if you kiss others too. Go
away—No, don't go ; you shall not go.'

' *Voilà* !' she answered, looking at me with
dancing eyes, ' the little one is jealous also.
He has inherited it.'

' Where are you going ? ' interrupted my
nurse, more sternly than I ever heard her
speak before.

' Going ? Oh, there are a hundred places

where I can go. I'm not so homeless as
madame thinks. I've got better blood in my
veins than she has. And *I* was never sold to
pay my father's debts. Oh, the grand name
Smythe! the lordly name of Smythe! *Cœur
chéri'*—and here she sank upon her knees
again—'I know who you are, and I'd rather
have a hair of your dear head than all their
riches.'

'You are a heap, heap better, Mamsell
Thérèse,' interposed William, 'than you'd
have us fur to think. Other folk builds
'emselves up, but you pulls yourself down
perpetual.'

'There you go again,' she cried, on her
feet like a flash of lightning. 'Why do you
make me bad when I am good? I want to be
good sometimes. I am a *méchante fille*, I
know it; yet sometimes I want to be good.'

She was crying loudly again, and William
was coughing, and there was a regular

hubbub in the nursery, for the baby had been awakened, and was joining lustily in the chorus. As for me, I naturally made what little noise I could, with my arms round Thérèse's waist, the while I told her, firstly, that she should never go, and then, that I would come after her and marry her and bring her back in triumph. I don't know what else I might have said but for a piece of toffy, exceedingly sticky, which was suddenly thrust into my mouth, and which completely disabled me. But I ran after them down into the hall, and saw Thérèse spring into the coach, and William get in after her, coughing still.

Then, just when I had abandoned hope, and made sure she wouldn't, Thérèse turned her lovely face and looked at me. All trace of grief had gone out of it, and it was bright and smiling. Nay, I am not quite sure that it was not full of fun at my expense. I heard a silvery laugh as they drove off, and a sweet fresh voice carolling a French *chanson*. I recognised the air, and even the words, long years afterwards.

'Tra, la, la,' sang Thérèse, with one breaking heart beside her and another breaking heart left behind :—

> 'Tra, la, la, la, la, la, la, la,
> L'Amour vous attend là.'

As if she knew, as if she ever could learn, the cruel enchantress, what Love meant!

CHAPTER III.

A COMMON PERSON BENEATH CRITICISM.

Es hört doch jeder nur, was er versteht.
GOETHE (*Sprüche in Prosa*).

ONLY a footman and a lady's-maid! for what
was Thérèse after all, in spite of her airs and
graces—what was she but a lady's-maid,
forced to brush my mother's hair, paint my
mother's face, submit to my mother's whims,
and take my mother's wages? What difference did it make that she could take a sweet
revenge along with these things, by many a
side glance over my mother's head into the
mirror, smiling a little as if she were triumphantly comparing nature and art?

Only a footman and a lady's-maid! while

I was Charles Reginald Smythe (with the Y,
remember!), only son to one of the richest
men in the City, and, as my father told me a
hundred times, getting on tip-toe to say it,
for he was but short and the sum vast and
majestic, heir to a million—me-illion!

Yet for all the apparent chasm between
us, the destinies of these two were irretriev-
ably interwoven with mine.   Fate plays us
queer tricks; sometimes making of our own
most cherished hopes knotted cords where-
with to scourge us; sometimes fashioning a
lifeboat of our fears, which may become our
only refuge from the shipwreck of our
hopes.

I was born in London, and if I may trust
my own memory in regard to that important
event, I was born in a row.   If you will not
trust my memory in this respect, you will
allow me to draw conclusions, I suppose, and
my conclusions all agree as to the extreme

probability of this premiss. For why else should rows from my very earliest infancy have come as natural to me as my bottle?

I suppose too that neither rows nor bottle agreed with me particularly. I think I ran the gauntlet of every disease incidental to childhood before I was two years old, having a very turbulent special row of my own with Death on each occasion. And I am quite sure that he, like my mother, would inevitably have had the best of it, but for one faithful champion who fought for me, and who would without the least hesitation have supplied a failing bolt to bar him out with her own tender arm, as another did before her.

Need I say that this champion was a woman? For it is the women alone who, doing some of the hardest and least rewarded work of this world, let others have the credit of it.

I was baptized in a row. The dispute as to whether my name should be Charles, after my father, or Reginald, after the hero of the last romance my mother had been reading, was continued even at the font, and only settled by the impatient clergyman, who cut the Gordian knot by christening me with both.

Thus I became duly registered and catalogued among my fellow-creatures, and in course of time grew into the knowledge that I was I—a little centre around which the universe naturally revolved.

Once—heaven knows what prompted me to the effort!—I tried to love my mother. I had got into her boudoir somehow, and was sitting on a low footstool near the couch on which she was reclining, watching her hand whereon diamonds glittered, as it lazily turned the pages of a novel she was reading. Her eyebrows were very black, and her cheeks very pink, and her lips even redder than those of Thérèse.

I sat there watching her, my heart growing fuller every moment, my lip beginning to tremble, as I thought of the Bible stories my nurse had told me—of Hagar and Ishmael, of Rebecca and Jacob, of Hannah and Samuel. Surely those veiling lids must cover eyes able to look at me differently than with the cold look to which I was accustomed ; surely the warm colour on the cheeks must be the reflex of something warmer underneath !

The next moment I was clinging to her, crying passionately, my wet lips on hers, the hot drops from my eyes washing away the rosy flush I had thought so beautiful, and revealing nothing underneath it but a cold and sickly pallor.

I never tried to love my mother again. She murdered even the wish as she threw me off and sat up upon the couch, her face ghastly pale except for patches of red upon her lips, and streaks of the same colour, fringed with yellow, on her cheek.

I was not crying as I scrambled to my feet again, though I had knocked my head against the footstool and bruised my arm. My white frock was crushed and stained, my curls were hopelessly out of order, and my cheek was burning, but I was not crying.

For a moment I stood and she sat, both of us looking at one another. Then I cried out to go back to my nurse, and she cried out to her maid to take me there. That night I woke up from sleep, trembling. Again I saw as in a vision the semblance of a woman's face crowned with a mountain of hair. Its colour was a sickly yellow stained with red ; its eyes were wide open and dilated—full of dread as if they were looking upon death. So they were—upon the corpse of filial love.

But that another supplied the places of

both father and mother, I should, in spite of
my heirship, have been a wretched little
pauper indeed.

She was nothing particular to look at, that
dear nurse of ours. A little woman, neat and
unpretending as a Quakeress, with the patient
peace in her face which you may oftenest see
in the face of such an one—peace which was
not the result of want of trial, but the result
of having come out of it. 'These are they
which came out of great tribulation.' Such
are the Bible words which recur to my
memory when I think of her.

For she *had* come out of it. The deep
lines in her face had been graven there by
sorrow, yet the peace spread over all made
them so beautiful that you would not willingly
have missed one. Her eyes were blue and
gentle, the smile in them softened by the
shadows of many shed tears; her mouth still
retained a nervous twitch which it had ac-

quired during some supreme trial; her hands were the large, strong hands of a worker; her hair of a pale yellow, soft as silk. This hair, I fancy, was something like a thorn in the flesh to her, it being in a constant state of rebellion against the severe discipline to which it was subjected. However determinately combed back in the mornings under the high mob cap she wore (in which cap, bluebottles used to get and hum, to my intense delight), towards afternoon and evening it would break into ripples, curling back in little rings over her broad low forehead in a way I used to think lovely. It was obstinate hair, and, like us children, wouldn't always be trained in the way it should go. Once, I remember, the baby pulled off her cap, and I fancy I see again now the torrent of sunshine which for a moment flooded the sedate shawl she wore crossed over her bosom.

This woman's name was Smith. She told

me this once herself in a little burst of emotion, and with an unusual flash in her gentle eye. And she added quickly that my grandfather had borne it with honour and left it unsullied. It had been good enough for him.

I inquired why it was not good enough for my father, being still too much of a child to comprehend the gulf which separates Smith from Smythe.

To which she gave a strange and curious answer, her mouth twitching in the old nervous way and with the same most unusual warmth.

' Let the cruel thing that weaned a brother from a sister answer that,' said she.

I pressed for a still further explanation, this being somewhat enigmatical.

Continuing the game of cross questions and crooked answers, she further remarked, sobbing now and strongly agitated, that it was offering up of own relations on the shrine of Mammoth (I think she said Mammoth, though I don't pretend to know what she meant), which somehow or other had resulted in Smythe, and finally she broke into a fit of crying, all the more terrifying because she cried so seldom, until it became quite as much as I could do to kiss her back to smiles again.

I remember that the smiles were very watery, and that the gentle bosom upon which I nestled was long agitated. When she put me to bed an hour afterwards, she herself joined audibly with me in one clause of the Lord's Prayer, repeating it with almost pas sionate earnestness. 'Forgive us our tres- passes,' we said together, ' as we forgive them that trespass against us.'

Even after she had said good-night and snugly tucked me up in my cot, she lingered musingly beside me, finally kneeling down again at the bedside to lay her head upon

the pillow close to mine; her hair hopelessly in confusion, her sunken cheek brightly
flushed, her gentle lip trembling. After a few
moments of silence she put her mouth close
to my ear, and whispered softly that I must
forget what she had said, that it was naughty
of her to have said it, and that she was sorry.
1 nearly had forgotten, in the interest of a
wonderful fairy story she had told me since,
probably for that very purpose, but this
remark of hers, well meant but injudicious—
the dear little woman was not wise in her
generation, being one of the children of light
—brought it all back again, investing it with
new importance. I fell asleep murmuring
her own words of an hour before :

'Let the cruel thing that weaned a brother
from a sister answer that.'

CHAPTER IV.

BALLYACORA HALL.

But the child's sob in the silence curses deeper
Than the strong man in his wrath.
                                    ELIZABETH B. BROWNING.

I WAS eight years old when we migrated to
Ballyacora Hall. Two or three other things
of almost equal importance occurred about
the same period. Firstly, I was promoted
to real trousers—*real* ones, like a man's.
Secondly, my curls were cut off. Thirdly, I
became owner of a live pony and a live groom,
both of whom could wince if I whipped 'em.
Hip, hip, hip !——

No, I can't for the life of me ! There was
a fourthly, which, like Aaron's rod, swallowed

up all the others, remaining afterwards as
lean and gaunt as ever.

I had to part with my nurse. All my
kickings and screamings and threatenings to
kill myself lost their potency on this occasion.
Why, I learnt afterwards.

Ballyacora Hall, County Cork, Ireland,
had become my father's in some mysterious
manner connected with a bankrupt lord,
with racecourses, and the devil to pay generally. I picked up this information from
scraps of talk which fell from the lips of my
elders, piecing them together, while pre-
serving every outward sign of complete
indifference.

I also found out in the same manner that,
though my maternal grandfather had certainly
been a baronet, that high-minded aristocrat
had not scrupled to allow his daughter to pay
his numerous debts in a way which *she* called
heroic, but which my father styled some-

thing very different.　And a very tough rod, fashioned out of this act, was in constant requisition by my parents for the chastisement of each other.

But in whatever way Ballyacora Hall became the property of my father, it certainly possessed eminently suitable qualities for making a gentleman of his heir.　It was so redolent of aristocratic perfume from cellar to attic that you couldn't live in it without imbibing its odour.　The wine vaults had formerly been dungeons, wherein kernes had been tortured to death, and there was a recess in the wall still which had once contained, so they said, a human skeleton.　Upstairs was an oaken chest, which smelt like a vault, and which had been the burial-place of a noble lady, nailed in there by an offended lord to die at her leisure.　And the banqueting, now the entrance, hall still reeked with the legends of former revellers, when the times were ' good old times,' and masters were masters and serfs serfs, and women creatures to be dealt with as men chose. What wonder that after sucking in such tales like mother's milk I went out among *my* dependents to swagger and hector and kick where I could—every evil instinct in me at its strongest, every good one dormant?

Thus I grew up to be fourteen years old, a big, handsome, headstrong boy; my only discipline an occasional thrashing from my father, at times when I deserved it least; my only mentor an occasional twinge from a conscience, which had been so tenderly fostered in my early childhood that no neglect would quite silence it now.

It was one of these twinges of conscience which sent me to the top of the house before my departure for Eton to say good-bye to my neglected sisters, who lived, or sickened and died, up there, out of sight and sound and hearing of the denizens below.

'Poor little wretches!' I thought, as I mounted stair after stair, 'what a deuce of a way to go up and come down! By the way, do they *ever* come down?'

And my heart swelled a little, half with pity, half with complacency at my own superior position—the boy who could not be ignored—the heir who would be lord of all.

I was directed in my search for the right room by a child's voice and the song of a canary. I opened the door, walked in un-announced, and stood among its inmates.

My abrupt entrance was the signal for a wild retreat on the part of several long-haired, short-frocked, bare-legged, sticky-mouthed atoms of feminine humanity to the protecting skirts of nurse. Only two remained stationary, the baby in the cradle, (even the slatternly nursemaid rocking it started up aghast at my unexpected appearance) and a little girl in a corner, who continued her singular occupation of tearing paper from the wall, with a nonchalance which surprised even me.

'Hullo!' I said, 'what's the row?'

(Rows came so natural to me, you know.)

The flock of timid sheep clustered round nurse, looked at me with wide blue eyes, but uttered not a word. The little girl in the corner laughed a harsh, disdainful laugh, most unchildlike.

'Oh, 'tis only that they're so naughty and so ill-behaved, sir,' said nurse, a gaunt, bony, scraggy-necked individual, with a sharp voice and sharp red nose. 'Nobody'd think as I took the pains with 'em I do, or that they was clean this morning. Hold your noise, you brute!' This last to the canary, which broke out into a shrill, sarcastic whistle.

Oh, how knowing that bird looked, to be sure! How artfully he cocked one bright eye,

first at me and then at nurse! How cun-
ningly he turned a pirouette on his perch,
coming up wrong side foremost and seeming
to be pantomimically saying with his quivering tail, ' Gammon, sir, gammon, all gammon!'

'That is a lie, Atkinson,' said the little girl
in the corner, quietly endorsing the canary,
the while she continued her occupation of
stripping the wall of its covering. ' You stayed
in bed this morning to breakfast and told Sally
to dress us, and Sally read her book and told
us to dress ourselves. That's the reason we
are so dirty, except Florry. Florry would be
clean in a pigstye.'

I don't think anyone in the room drew
breath for a few seconds after this speech, except perhaps the baby. I'm sure the canary
didn't, for he stood motionless on his perch,
his head drawn into his body and every
feather in him standing out as straight as an
arrow. I'm sure *I* didn't either, for the look

nurse directed towards the back of the daring
little speaker was almost murderous.

' Is it me or Miss Mabel that's telling a
lie?' she gasped, turning to another of the
children, whom, if I hadn't known it before, I
should still have recognised as Florence from
her sister's last words. Her pinafore was the
only unsoiled one in the room, her trousers
were the only ones frilled. Her snowy neck
and shoulders, soft, dimpled hands, and rose-
tinted cheeks seemed unsoilable. I noticed
too that her long, rich brown curls were carefully brushed and tied back with a ribbon.
It was evident that whether anybody else took
care of her or not, Florence would take care
of herself. She stood among the others, un-
stained and soilless, like a delicate hothouse
flower among weeds.

' Is it me or is it Miss Mabel?' repeated
the nurse.

I watched Florry's blue-veined lids fall

over her bluer eyes, and saw the rose-tint on her cheek deepen a little.

'Florry will say what you wish,' broke in again that fearless voice from the corner; 'she is afraid of being beaten else, or having her ribbon taken away, and Florry loves her own comfort and fine clothes better than the truth. I used to be afraid of you too, but I'm not now.   I've made you afraid of me.'

'Come out of that corner this minute,' said nurse, now too furious to conceal her wrath any longer.   'Of all spiteful, impish——'

'Go on,' said the voice; 'let Charley hear you, and the nice words you teach us. I'll come out of the corner when I choose; you put me here for your pleasure, and I shall stay for mine.'

It was time to put an end to the scene, for nurse's wrath was changing from hot to cold, and a strangled sob made me think with terror of my mother's hysterics.   I put out my hand

and drew one of the weeds towards me—a
pretty weed with innocent eyes, a rosebud of
a mouth, extremely dirty, and a quantity of
rough, unkempt yellow hair hanging behind
it. This weed, which had a chubby thumb in
its mouth, was my favourite among them—
little Irish Aileen.

'Come,' I said coaxingly, 'you'll talk to
me, won't you? I'm going away to school,
and I sha'n't see you again for ever so long.
What's the matter? You know who I am,
don't you?'

If Aileen's thumb had been soluble, it must
have disappeared before my eyes, she sucked
it so vigorously.

'Miss Aileen, you naughty girl, take your
thumb out of your mouth and answer your
brother,' said nurse, glad to find a less dangerous victim, ' or——'

The ' or ' was sufficient. The thumb came
out with a sound like a cork from a bottle,

and Aileen's cherub lips opened to a lisping
' Yeth.'

'Who am I, then? Don't be frightened,'
I said encouragingly.

Renewed hesitation, renewed impetus, and
the answer came forth again with a burst :

' Master Charles.'

'What a silly little girl you are! Say
'' Charles." '

' Nurse talls you Master Charles, and says
she would like to have the trimming of you.'

' Nurse is only a servant—only a common
servant,' I replied indignantly, ' but you will
be a lady. She calls you *Miss* Aileen too,
doesn't she ? '

' Thometimes '—this with a pressure of
the baby lips, which shows me that, though
Aileen can be awed by nursery discipline, she
is still capable of revolt against it—'and
thometimes hussy, and chit, and 'ittle yetch.'

Aileen is not such a heroine as that other

weed in the corner. Her courage is of a true
feminine order; capable of audacious daring,
but rapidly sinking afterwards into profound
dismay at its own act. She drew nearer to
me as she spoke, and put her little hand upon
my shoulder.

'Never mind,' I said, breaking the succeeding silence by an embarrassed laugh.
'Tell me what I shall bring you when I
come home for the holidays. What would
you like, Florence? Speak. You are the
eldest.'

Florence's blue eye brightened, her breath
came a trifle quicker, the lovely colour on her
cheek deepened again.

'Well?'

'A pink frock, trimmed with lace,' she
said eagerly.

'Our last kitten was black, and not all
the soap in the world could wash it white,'
broke in that uncanny voice from the corner.

'But we never tried,' said innocent Aileen ;
' bethides, it would have hurt it.'

'And what would you like, Mabel?' I
asked, and I waited with curiosity for the
answer.

For the first time since I entered the room
Mabel turned so that we could see her face.
I had often seen it before, of course, but
I saw it now with opened eyes and awakened
understanding. There was no beauty in it.
The forehead was too broad and pronounced
for a girl, the temples too bare and promi-
nent. Even the keen, sarcastic grey eye
looked more dangerous than attractive ; there
was a sparkle in it, sharp as the edge of a
knife. Her scanty brown hair was close-
cropped like a boy's, her long nose slightly
crooked ; round her thin straight mouth were
lines that would have looked premature in a
woman of thirty. Her mouth was expanded
and her forehead contracted, yet she was

neither smiling nor frowning as she answered
me.

'What is it to be, Mabel?'

'A rod for a fool's back,' said the strange
girl.

I don't know why I coloured, nor why I
fancied that these words were aimed with
special intention, and that their aim was myself. As if the child knew what she was talking about! Then I turned to Aileen.

'Now, my pet, what is your choice?

'Can I have what I want most?'

'Yes, what you want most.'

There was a curious agitation in Aileen's
little throat, and her blue eyes were filled with
tears, and her round mouth was quivering.

'Don't cry. You ain't going to cry, are
you? Tell me what you want most.'

If there had been a recording angel present,
he would have had a heavy reckoning to set
against my mother's name that moment. The

look on the child's face was full of infinite pathos and infinite reproach.

She put her arms around my neck and her wet cheek close to mine, and whispered so low that no one else could hear:

'Bring me back a new mamma.'

If there had been a recording angel present, no tear, no ocean of tears, could have blotted out *that* indictment.   I had a boy's heart, tough and unimpressible, but the words fell heavy upon it; they left an indelible wound there, which is angry and throbs still.

I went away soon after that, after having distributed my sweets and kissed each dirty little mouth, save one.   I could not kiss Florence; she had advanced towards me with so much graceful dignity, that I made her as awkward a bow as I should have done to a grown lady.

Nurse accompanied me to the door, once more as sweet and slimy as butter-scotch,

as mellow as toffy. ' How Miss Mabel do put
me out to be sure!' she said ; 'but there, I
never bear malice. My bark's worse than my
bite any day.'

I made no response. When she shut the
door I remained a moment on the landing,
but there was no sound inside, save the creak-
ing of the cradle and the song of the canary.
Yet there was an oppressive feel in the silence
quite the reverse of reassuring.

I had ascended the stairs with a vague
expectation of finding three or four feminine
creatures there, looking a little different
outwardly but as like as peas within. I had
imagined sweets and dolls in the present,
dresses and lovers in the future, to be the
summit of their ambition. Yet even in that
neglected garden each plant was growing
according to its nature. Culture might make
an apple of the crab, a plum of the sloe, a
garden of the hedge-side rose, but it was

powerless to induce the bramble-bush to put forth figs, or the fig-tree brambles. The characters of those three sisters of mine were as different as if they had not sprung from the same root and been cultivated in the same soil—nay, as different as if they had been masculine instead of feminine. My thoughts were crude enough, but I pondered over these things.

I had found one sister capable of vanity, one capable of sarcasm, one capable of love.

' A rod for a fool's back.' Who was rod and who was fool? Nonsense, pure folly!

Yet the words haunted me, recurring again and again like a prophecy.

CHAPTER V.

LIFE AND ITS ATTRACTIONS.

Only deeds give life its strength, and only moderation its charm.—JEAN PAUL.

THE next day I left home for Eton, went through the usual courses of fagging and flogging there, picked up some scraps of knowledge, the most important of which was perhaps that I was by no means universally acknowledged as the centre of the universe, and finally, after being, as I congratulate myself, rather brilliantly plucked at Oxford after a few years' residence there, came home to celebrate my majority.

That over, and the discovery made that my sisters were growing into remarkably fine girls ; that there was no other fine girl circulating round, not a sister, available for a preliminary flirtation; that my father was balder, greyer, and more plebeian-looking than ever; and that my mother was having the worst of it in her daily contest with age, I came to the definite conclusion that Ballyacora was the dullest place in creation, and life there insupportable.

This result I communicated in the best of good faith to my father, almost as soon as it was arrived at.

We were alone together in his *sanctum sanctorum*, euphemistically called 'the study,' though the only subject studied there was £ s. d.—debit and credit. I was lounging in his easy-chair, the while he stood before me, my sensitive university nose wrinkling in undisguised disgust at the tradesman-like atmosphere of the place, my sensitive hands thrust deep down into my trouser-pocke for fear of contamination.

'I can't stand this humdrum place any longer,' I said. 'I want to see life and to enjoy it.'

'And so you shall, Charley,' said my father, 'so you shall.'

There was something in the tone of his voice as he spoke which startled me and made me look up; something as if two voices belonging to two people had melted into one. And yet, though melted, they were separate still, and discordant, and not in unison.

There was also a double expression in his face as I looked at it. The one half, the usual and dominant expression—the other, a latent and concealed one, long kept in the background, but now breaking irresistibly forth in futile yet hot rebellion.

And for a moment I recognised the old English oak cracking the varnish which would fain have concealed its existence—the true among the false, his heirloom and mine,

inherited from a long line of noble an-
cestors.

'So you shall,' he said, 'on one condition.'

'What is that?'

'You are my only son,' he continued,
wiping his face with a red and yellow silk
handkerchief, as if conscious that it was
eloquent on its own account and had better
be silenced, 'and are heir to a million—a
me-illion.'

I had heard this so often that it seemed
as natural and as immutable a law of the
universe as that my hair was blond and
curly, that my mother read novels perpetually, that the girls were of no importance
as compared to me, and that the earth
revolved round the sun.

'A me-illion,' he continued, one hand on
the bulging pocket of his coat, the other
jingling loose coin in his breeches pockets,

' wasn't earned in a day, no, nor in a month either, nor without sleepless nights and anxious days, and tears of blood, and indignities without number, and insults to be stored up and paid back with usury.'

As he withdrew his hand from the bulging pocket to draw forth the red and yellow pocket handkerchief again, I almost heard the varnish creak, it split so furiously; as he wiped away some moisture which had gathered in his eyes, I think that if my moral nature had not been so warped and poisoned, and he the poisoner, I should almost have respected him. As it was, the emotion which for a moment contracted my throat was gone as he revarnished himself and revarnished me.

' What is the condition?' I asked carelessly.

But though I asked, I knew well enough what he meant. It had been talked about a

hundred times. Even the babies in the
nursery must have known that I was destined
to marriage with a duke's daughter; to scale
the summit of the aristocratic ladder which
my father had striven so unsuccessfully to
mount himself.

And I was satisfied on the whole with this
condition. I would do what he wished.
Only not now, not now! I must have my fling
first.

'I've sweated and toiled all for you, my
boy,' he went on. 'To make a gentleman of
you has been the aim of my life. I was not
always Smythe of Ballyacora. And if the
place is dull to you, don't you think it's dull
to me? don't you think I want a bit of change
sometimes? But I'm willing to give up everything else for the sake of the one thing I've
set my heart upon. Look at you there, young,
rich, handsome, clever—a match for anyone!'

He was looking at me with pride and

affection, and yet his look did not soften, it only hardened me. For my thoughts had sprung back with a sudden rebound to long-forgotten memories. I saw another face, something like his and yet so different, and heard a voice saying, 'Let the cruel thing that weaned a brother from a sister answer that.'

'You *shall* see life,' he said, 'see it at your leisure and with full pockets. I can wait another year or two. And then, my boy, you will come back to fulfil my life's desire and take my place in Ballyacora Hall.

'I have always done my duty by you,' he concluded pompously, 'and I shall expect you then to do your duty by me.'

If occasionally licking me, not for my benefit, but his own relief, if pampering every bad thing within me, if stifling my conscience and pauperising my heart, had been doing that duty, so he had—so he had. As for mine

to him, had he never read those divine words:
' What a man soweth, that shall he also
reap ? '

So we separated. I went upstairs to make
preparation for my speedy departure from
Ballyacora, aided or hindered therein by
Aileen, who persisted in wasting oceans of
love upon me in spite of my meagre acknow-
ledgment of the same, while he remained
behind, either engrossed in the absorbing
study of £ s. d. or brooding over his parental
programme and its approaching consummation.

But, lack-a-day ! Fate sometimes plays the
dickens with parental programmes.

.   .   .   .   .

I had written to some Oxford friends of
mine—friends after my father's own heart, for
they were both noble, I mean *titled*—and
informed them that I was coming up to
London to see life in their company. After
which I dutifully went again to my father's

study to receive from him certain pieces of paper and his blessing ; thrashed Patsey, my groom, to make him remember, and handsomely tipped him to make him forget ; ran up to my mother's boudoir to kiss her, stage-fashion, both of us simultaneously saluting the air ; rubbed my sprouting moustache against Aileen's wet little face ; and departed in high feather, leaving the dullest place in creation and my own destiny behind me for an indefinite period. To youth to-day is everything ; to-morrow, something so far removed as hardly to be worth taking into consideration.

Well, I saw life in the company of these noble friends, both of whom sought to find some new bloom upon it from the freshness of their companion—saw it, at first, with eager curiosity, quaffing cup after cup of its pleasures with all the insatiability of immaturity ; then suddenly 1 came to the dregs, and the swallowing of them sickened me.

There was nothing worth living for in
England : that was as clearly evident to me
as that Ballyacora was the dullest place in
creation. Again I tried to turn my back
upon myself, forgetting that whithersoever I
went I must carry it with me.

'It's *une grande passion* you need,' said
the nobler of my two noble friends, Lord
George Graceless, who was himself *tout épris*,
as he called it, with one of the ladies of the
ballet. (My other noble friend, Sir Harry
Goitt, was already gone—to the dogs.)

'I'll go abroad,' I said, 'and try life
there.'

'If it wasn't for Celestine, I'd go with
you,' sighed his lordship. 'They understand
how to live better than we do, over there in
France.'

So I went to France, carrying my malady
with me, for I could not leave myself behind.

And I went to Austria and Spain, and

finally to Italy, seeking what I could not find
—an illusive something which ever danced
before me, and the futile search for which
led me deeper and deeper into the marshes.

At last, weary and hopeless, I crossed the
mountain barrier and descended into Switzerland.

I would spend a few days here, I thought,
to try and believe in Nature, if I could, after
having lost all faith in man. I wandered on
among defiles and over mountains, looking
up to the snowy summits, all turned towards
God, hoping that up there at least was purity,
long since vanished, alas! from every spot
nearer earth.

It was an evening early in September and
the sun was setting, when I reached Lucerne.
The promenade beside the lake was thronged
with admiring spectators, amongst whom I
wandered listlessly and hopelessly. There
were people of all nations among the crowd.

Ever and anon I caught scraps of English, French, German, and Italian.

The setting sun, dying in a lake of blood behind Mount Pilate, bathed the world in a crimson flood and heated red-hot with its fiery breath the top of every mountain. Mount Pilate itself, clothed sumptuously in purple and fine linen, was beginning to reflect the light of a gentler monarch now that the more ardent one was departing. Already the moon's young crescent, pale with envy, sent a silvery messenger over the snow to herald his coming ; already the deep blush on the mountains was paling, and the gold on the rippling water at my feet changing into silver.

I was listlessly wondering which was the more beautiful, the passion of the moment before or the purity of the present. I was leaning on the parapet and looking down into the dazzling water, when a lady's dress swept lightly over my foot, the lace on a lady's mantle tickled my hand, and a lady's soft warm breath mingled itself with the breath of Nature upon my cheek.

I had been crowded, hustled, run against, pushed aside a hundred times this evening already, and why these gentle touches should have affected me so powerfully, I cannot tell. I only know that they ran through me like a succession of electric shocks, and that every nerve in my body throbbed a response to them. I looked round.

Close beside me stood a lady and beyond her a gentleman. Both were leaning, as I was, upon the parapet which protects the promenade towards the lake. Both were apparently occupied, as I was, in contemplating the wondrous landscape before us, which Nature had just been freshly colouring into a glory unspeakable.

CHAPTER VI.

PRINCE AND DAME DE COMPAGNIE

Who hath not found himself surprised into revenge, or
action, or passion, for good or evil, whereof the seeds lay within
him, latent and unsuspected, until the occasion called them
forth?—THACKERAY (*Esmond*).

BUT appearances may be deceitful. The pair
beside me, both wonderfully handsome, both
evidently struggling with a supreme emotion,
were as indifferent to the beauty of the scene
before them as if they had been blind. They
were gazing, not at it, but, intently at one
another.

Yet that she was looking at him could
only be guessed at by the expression in his
face, turned towards me. It was lit up by

the last sun ray, and was all aflame with
passion and anger and love and entreaty and
fury at the opposition which he seemed to
read in hers, and fierce intention to over-
come it.

How can I describe him—the man whom
I instinctively felt was destined to become my
arch-enemy—the man whom I was fated to
hunt down unto his death ?

At the very moment when I had finally
discovered that life was not worth the living,
Fate lit up two fires in my heart, which for a
long time burned with almost equal intensity
—fires fundamentally opposed, and yet continually fed the one by the other—love and
hate.

That he would be no despicable enemy was
apparent at the first glance.   His rank was evidently far beyond my own.   His beauty was
so extraordinary that as I gazed I saw others
gaze too in open-eyed admiration.

' What a magnificent man!' whispered an English lady passing us.

' *Mon Dieu! quelle beauté superbe!*' murmured a Frenchman.

' *Donnerwetter! welch ein Paar!*' cried an enthusiastic German.

Whether these remarks were heard or not by the object of them, I cannot say. His deep, dark, heavily-fringed blue eyes remained fixed upon the lady's face; his beautifully-cut, transparent nostrils still quivered; between his full, red, haughtily-curled lips his white teeth gleamed—like those of some magnificent, ferocious wild animal; and through the rich brown of his complexion you might still see the hot Southern blood palpitate. When at last he spoke I drew my breath to listen, bending my head low over the water as if that were the sole object of my thoughts.

His voice corresponded to his appearance.

perfectly. It was soft, musical, seductive, passionate, and commanding all in one. Through every word he uttered ran a threat which seemed to say, ' Yield, or I will compel thee. Resist, and I will oppose the strength of my manhood to the weakness of thy womanhood, and kill if I cannot conquer thee.'

I saw the woman shudder as he broke the spell which had bound her, and saw too the look with which he stilled and silenced her, awing even the fibres of her body into submission.

' Käthe,' he said (I understood enough German to be able to follow him), ' *Mädchen, entschliesse dich doch. Glaubst du etwa dass meine Geduld ewig dauern wird?'* (Make up your mind. Do you think my patience will last for ever?)

She made no answer, except by a quick motion of her hand, meant to indicate, I believe, that there was some one near who might hear and heed him. It is a singular characteristic of women that they never, even at the most critical moment, lose their innate fear of exposure, although men under the same circumstances forget it utterly.

Her companion turned his wonderful eyes, with their attractive yet steely glitter, full on me for a moment, then lowered them contemptuously.

'Bah,' he muttered, '*ein verrückter Engländer*' (a crazy Englishman). 'He'll understand no other language than his own accursed one.'

I felt flattered, of course, so flattered that I ground my teeth, cursing him through them, and laid my hand involuntarily upon the hilt of a short Italian dagger I kept in my pocket. But I listened on, restraining myself for the present, my tell-tale eyes upon the water.

'Käthe,' he said again, and through the

music of his voice ran the same chord of
threatening, 'speak, speak quickly, and say,
"Eberhard, my Eberhard, I will yield, I will
do what thou wishest," or, *bei Gott!* I shall
kill thee or kill myself. I cannot endure
this uncertainty any longer, *denn ich habe
dich lieb. Gerechter Himmel!* until now I
scorned the passion, lighting up its flame in
the hearts of others and laughing as it consumed them!'

The fierceness of his manner as he spoke,
the brutality of the passion which flashed out
of his eyes, his profane use of the tender
German words: *Ich habe dich lieb*—words
almost more sweetly simple than our English
'I love you'—maddened me into a fury as un-
controllable as it was unreasonable. As crazy
for the moment as he had insultingly called
me, I turned fiercely towards him, my hand
again upon the hilt of my dagger, at the
sharp point of which my hatred seemed to

concentrate itself, and to become deadly, and to lust for blood.

'*Der gnädige Herr verzeihen*,' I said, ironically using the most deferential form of words I could find, ' but I am neither so crazy nor so ignorant as you seem to imagine. I perfectly understand what you have been saying, and—and——'

The passion which was consuming me consumed my voice too, and prevented my finishing what I had to say. His haughty eyes met mine once more, this time a faint shadow of surprise modifying their brilliancy.

'Very well, sir,' he answered, speaking slowly, but in very excellent and refined English, 'and what then? You have a right to understand, of course, but gentlemen do not listen.'

The hot blood, which instantly dyed my face scarlet, pleaded guilty to the charge he implied, and maddened me still further. He smiled sarcastically as he turned from me to his companion again. She had slightly moved. and I could see the lovely contour of her face, and the slow tears which were falling one by one into the water.

'Come, Käthe,' he said, 'let us go.'

'Not yet, sir,' I cried, casting prudence. forethought, everything but wild passion, to the wind. 'You have twice deliberately insulted me. I call you to account for it. I demand satisfaction.'

The contemptuous look with which he now regarded me from head to foot was worse than a blow—worse than a blow in the eyes of all the populace. Then he stooped to the lady, uttering a few rapidly-spoken words in a language quite new to me. She rose instantly from her leaning position on the parapet, still keeping her face averted, and they moved slowly away together; his spurred heels (he was attired in the closely-fitting rich uniform of a foreign cavalry officer) seeming to spurn the ground they touched; his long sword clattering noisily after him upon the pavement.

'Sir,' I said, quickly following and trying to speak with dignity and calmness, 'here is my card. You will give me yours in return if you please, and we can settle this matter at a more convenient season.'

He took my card, glanced at the name upon it with that curling back of his full red lips which made him look so like a magnificent wild animal, and said in a sharp, clear voice, and in words of which every one struck and hurt me:

'I am staying at the hotel L'Impératrice d'Autriche. If you will call there to-morrow morning I will give orders that my courier and *maître d'affaires*, Monsieur de Laffolie, shall give you audience. He will be quite ready to show you what weapon we use in my country for chastising the impertinences of boys. Not the sword, *Herr je!* but the horsewhip, my young sir, or the cane.'

As he uttered these insulting words he tore my card in two, flung it over the parapet into the water, and strode forward again, leaving me with the boiling passion in my heart stilled into that intense quiet which is the beginning of murder.

What I should have done next I know not—I had already drawn my dagger from its sheath—when the lady turned and looked at me, her lovely eyes first full of terrified caution, rapidly changing into profound surprise and eager curiosity.

O, those eyes and that face! and, above all, that incomprehensible expression! Had she seen me before, or I her, or had we both known and loved one another in a dream?

I do not know when I became aware that I was the centre of attraction for many curious eyes. I remember hearing again the words which had formed an excuse for my first outbreak of fury. '*Ach, ein verrückter Engländer!*' the people cried, forming a dense crowd around the place where I stood. '*Ein verrückter Engländer!*' the burly gendarme echoed, as he forced his way through the gaping multitude and bore down heavily upon me.

CHAPTER VII.

UN GRAND PETIT HOMME.

For we are all so heavily weighted by the laws and conditions of the present ordered time, that no one, be he never so free, can long remain upright, without the support of a business or the excitement of a love affair.—IMMERMANN (*Münchausen*).

IN another moment I became aware that I was not only a laughing-stock for the public, but also in a confounded pickle. The gendarme's heavy hand was on my shoulder, his red face and flaming moustache in threatening proximity to mine, and his husky voice of authority in my ears, bidding me hand over the dagger I still brandished and follow him. · I knew that opposition would be worse than useless, and might be punished by long months of *Arrest*.

But before I had time to consider what I should do, the hand of the incorruptible officer of the law loosened its grasp of my shoulder to grasp something else ; his ferocious moustache suddenly grew quite amicable ; his left hand, palm outwards, deferentially touched the side of his official hat ; and leaving me, the offender, unmolested, he began soundly to rate the unoffending bystanders for blocking up the way.

While I gazed and wondered, half believing myself deluded by some vision, the dagger I still held was drawn gently from my clenched fist and replaced in its sheath.

Looking round amazed, I met a caustic, curious ray, darting out from the deep-set eyes of a little wiry Frenchman.

'Pardon, monsieur,' he said, with the national shrug of the shoulder, the national politeness, and the national grimace, 'I have fear that I have permitted myself to take too great a liberty, *mais*—ah, monsieur, you have much of—vat you call it?—plock, plock *anglais*, but it values better to have a little of discretion, a little of patience with the aristocrats.'

His voice began softly, rising at the end of each clause into the sing-song emphasis of 'the world's city.' His shabby clothes, too, had been made in Paris, and, though rubbed and worn at the seams, had a Parisian jaunti- ness about them still. His umbrella, a cheap one of cotton, was rolled into the smallest compass possible, and the toes of his shining boots reflected the crescent moon as if they had been mirrors.

'Was it you who sent away the gen- darme? Did you hear what that—that devil said to me?' I gasped. 'Do you know him?'

'The gendarme?—*mais oui*, monsieur; a very worthy citizen of Lucerne.'

'With a weakness for *les pourboire*.'

'You have said it, monsieur. But who has not his little weaknesses? Behold mine,' showing his shining boots.

'I did not mean him, though.'

'I have divined that also. You will say the other.'

'I mean the other.'

'And you called him *de dayvil.* You have well said, monsieur; it is the truth.'

'Do you know him too?'

'*Si*, monsieur, I know him. I know him well, and I mean, I, to know him better.'

The sparkle was gone from his eye, leaving it dark and menacing; his teeth met and moved slowly over one another like the grinding-stones of a mill; the light on his brightly polished boots changed from white to dull red, and looked like spots of blood.

'Where is he staying?' I asked. 'What is his name?'

All the music and the bright crescendo were gone from the Frenchman's voice as he answered me.

'He is staying at the hotel L'Impératrice d'Autriche, and his name is Monsieur le Prince de Pöbeldowski.'

'Is he there alone?'

'He is there with Madame la Princesse and suite.'

'You do not mean to say that the lady is —that he is married?' I faltered, something putting an icy hand on my heart and congealing its current.

'The lady with him is only the *dame de compagnie* of Madame la Princesse,' answered my companion, eyeing me keenly, 'and is poor and *bourgeoise*, I believe. *N'importe*; she is beautiful as an angel. I am old now, but I have been young too *dans le temps. Mon Dieu!* what hair! shining like pure gold. What eyes! no sky of summer was ever half so blue.   What *teint!* white and pure as the snow upon the tops of the mountains.'

He paused, watching me and the betraying hue upon my face, then went on :

'If I were young, instead of old, I would revenge myself on the aristocrat by entering the lists against him and bearing off the prize he is burning to win for himself. The prize may be honest as well as beautiful— *par ma foi, je le crois!*—may prefer marriage with a *bourgeois* to a liaison with a prince.'

I remembered the terror-stricken expression on the lovely face when it was turned towards him ; I saw again the eager, curious, interested look upon it when it was turned towards me. And suddenly life assumed a new aspect, became filled to the brim with a new desire, to the realisation of which I vowed to devote it.

'*Ecoutez,*' said the Frenchman, as we

moved away from the crowd, 'I am going to help you. *Halte là!* there is no reason for that vehement outburst of gratitude, because I am helping myself first. Only the good God knows for how many, many of days I have searched for an ally in vain. I, I also have a little account to settle with Monsieur le Prince.'

'You are a gentleman,' I said eagerly; 'be my second in this affair. I will kill him, or, by Jove, he shall kill me.'

'*Tiens! tiens!* Behold your English plock! Nevertheless it is you who would be killed, monsieur. Though he would not fight with you. A prince will not fight with a commoner.'

'By Jupiter Ammon, I'll make him, or show him that I too can handle a whip.'

Again the Frenchman's teeth met—this time sharply and savagely. Again his voice had lost its melodious ring when he spoke

' A whip—*un fouet—bon!* We will not forget that either. It too must have its place in our programme. But we have learned—we other Frenchmen—to go softly, to bide our time, to use the subterfuges. *Et le temps, le temps de vengeance viendra!*'

He lifted his dark eyes to the peaceful evening sky wherein the young moon now rode in all her glory, and murmured something which sounded like ' Gracieuse.' For a few minutes we walked on in silence.

' You will succeed, monsieur,' he continued. ' Something tells me that you will succeed if you will only let me help you. And it is not only the vengeance that I seek—is it not a good work to rescue the innocent?'

He seemed to find his answer in the stars, towards which he turned his eyes again. He seemed to be satisfied with that answer too, as he turned them back towards me.

' You have seen, monsieur,' he continued,

'how her blood rushes back affrighted to her heart when he even looks at her. And I have seen her walk alone beside the lake, looking into it, as if only under its water she knew where to turn for safety.'

There was nothing now but compassion in the dark eyes of my companion. I took his hand; I grasped it firmly in my own.

'You shall lead and I will follow,' I said; 'you shall be my captain, and I will be your lieutenant and aide-de-camp. As for the prize when it is won, we will——'

'Divide it?' he inquired, with an expressive French grimace. 'In the meantime leave my hand unmaimed, *mon lieutenant.* Ouf! That was the grip of a lion! Permit me to embrace you, French fashion, in return.'

French fashion did not quite accord with my British notions, but I submitted to it nevertheless.

'Behold one fact accomplished,' he cried

vivaciously. ‘ This evening Fate is smiling on us both. I—I have found an ally ; young, eager, vigorous. And you, *mon ami*, you have found something to do.’

Something to do. How did *he* know of the malady which was sapping my life-springs ? Yet how different life looked now to what it had done an hour before ! The blood ran swiftly, almost joyously, through the veins that had been so stagnant. My heart beat high and vigorously. Over a dark horizon a bright star had arisen.

‘ We will begin at once,’ I said.

‘ We will begin at once, monsieur. But you must first know who I am before en-rolling yourself under my banner. Will you see it ? I always carry it with me.’

He drew a small leather case out of his pocket, opened it, and held it before my as-tonished eyes. It was a piece of blue ribbon, stained with dull red marks. Upon it were stitched a few snow-white hairs. Underneath was written in red ink the one word: ' Gracieuse.'

CHAPTER VIII.

GRACIEUSE.

Qui veut voyager loin ménage sa monture.
                    RACINE (*Les Plaideurs*).

MY curiosity was strongly excited. I urged him to begin.

Let me tell the story again, translated from his own words, every syllable of which seemed graven on my heart as he poured it forth in the silvery moonlight. How strangely it contrasted with the peace of Nature ! The placid water rippled at our feet, pale lights twinkled feebly in the city behind us, the young moon hung motionless in a cloudless heaven, the solemn mountains had drawn fog-mantles over their ears, and seemed to repose. Every-

thing around appeared silently protesting
against our disturbing human element and
intrusion of human passion into the stillness
of the passionless night.

'I live in Lucerne, monsieur,' began the
Frenchman. 'I have already lived here
many years. There are reasons why I cannot return to my beloved France, my poor
Napoleon-ridden country—political reasons,
monsieur. Do not fear. I am an honest
man.'

Every line in his face—and there were
many—had told me that already.

'It was last autumn, monsieur, when that
happened about which I am going to tell
you. It is not a great thing—you may think
it very insignificant when you have heard
it. But *n'importe*, I will tell it you all the
same.

'Monsieur de Pöbeldowski was also here,
as now, with his mother, Madame la Prin-

cesse, and suite, only it was another *dame de compagnie*—not this one. I knew him well by sight. Who, having once seen him, could fail to know him again? I think if the arch-fiend could ascend from his infernal kingdom, clothed in every bit of masculine beauty conceivable, he would look like that man.'

I assented. The Frenchman had found a fit comparison.

'I lodge in a humble apartment *au rez-de-chaussée*, monsieur, with a widow who doubtless takes as good care of me as I deserve. For if her attentions are meagre and her reproaches munificent, who am I that I should complain?

'It was a very hot night in August, now more than a year ago. I had sunk to sleep after much uneasy tossing to and fro, but no sooner had I lost consciousness than I found it again. Something sobbing at my bedside caused me to spring up in a fright.

'I was half awake and half asleep, and I thought it was my little sister, who had died, poor little one, at the fête of the Virgin, which was her own fête too, for we had called her Gracieuse Marie after the blessed Mother of God. I put out my hand and laid it on her soft, warm, curly head, and cried, " *Gracieuse, ma petite! sois tranquille: c'est moi.*"

'Then I awoke a little more, and remembered how we had laid her in her last bed, dressed in the pretty frock she had worn at the fête, white, with blue ribbons, the Virgin's colours, and I sat up all trembling and said, "It is a spirit, and it no doubt betokens my death."

'It would have been quite dark in my room, for the night was sulphurous and heavy, but for the rays of a lamp outside in the street My window was open—I had forgotten to shut it—and I arose in order to do so, and to see what was beside me, whether spirit or

living thing. But I only saw my own white
face in a mirror, and the trembling of a tassel
hanging from my *bonnet de nuit*, and I heard
nothing save the beating of my own frightened
heart.

'"Pooh ! " I said, " a nightmare !—*rien de
plus !*" I mixed and drank to the dregs a
strong glass of *eau sucrée*, readjusted my
bonnet de nuit, glanced down the deserted
street, shut my window, and crept into bed
again. " There's a storm brewing over Mount
Pilate," I muttered ; "I might have known
yester-evening he wouldn't unsheath his
sword for nothing. It is well I awoke, or I
should have got hot ears in the morning for
letting in the rain."

'In spite of the *eau sucrée*, that strong
sedative, monsieur, I tossed and turned, seeking sleep in vain on the right hand and on the
left. At last I tried what lying still would
do, and with one result, at least. I heard the

sobbing again, and now I was wide awake.
There *was* some one in the room.

'That wasn't a burglar behind the door, it
was only my own coat and pantaloons, and
those boots were mine too—nobody else's were
ever half so bright. And besides, what had
I got for any burglar to steal, except some
shabby clothes and this umbrella and a cup
of *tisane* in the cupboard? I broke that cup
looking for him there, and came to myself
in the dismay of remembering that Madame
Papillote (that's my hostess) was taking care
of the remnant of my half-yearly pension, and
would also take good care to make me
liberally pay for the damage.

' Besides — though that was the last
thought of all—I remembered that a burglar
was hardly likely to begin his work by sobbing.'

' So you found nothing?'

' Your question savours of impatience,

monsieur; you doubtless think that I am
unusually old and garrulous; nevertheless if
I am to tell my tale at all I must tell it in
my own way. Yes, I did find something. I
heard a movement under the bed, valiantly
put in my hand, which rested again on something warm and soft and curly, and drew
forth——'

He stood still, turning his head to look at
me. I stood still too, looking at him.

' Ah, monsieur, you were smiling just
now at my long-windedness, and I smiled too,
yet some smiles are as mirthless as the lightning flash which momentarily lights up a
deep well of tears. My heart is full of tears
now as it was then, when I remember the poor
suffering creature which whined as I touched
it, and pitifully licked my hand and its own
bleeding wounds, looking up at me the while
with soft, dark, imploring eyes, for all the
world like those of my lost Gracieuse.

'Ah, monsieur, it seems to me that those
who can bear to hurt the beautiful living
things which God gave us will be punished
hereafter with the heaviest punishment He
has to inflict. I would rather have to answer at the great judgment seat for many a
crime which men deem mortal than for one
cruel act to a helpless thing put into my
power.'

'It was only a dog then?' I said, half dis-
appointed, half uneasy.

'Only a dog, monsieur. A little dog whose
long, silky hair was as white as the dress in
which we buried my Gracieuse. Round its
neck was a blue leather collar, upon which
was worked in raised gold a princely coronet
and the letter P. But now everything was
stained with blood—clotted blood, which
clung to my hands and to my *robe de chambre,*
and seemed to get inside me somehow and
cling to my heart.

'Listen, monsieur. I knew the dog belonged to Monsieur de Pöbeldowski, and I knew too—I knew it by instinct—that it was he who had beaten it to death. There were plenty of rumours concerning him floating about Lucerne, and not a few of them had penetrated even to my humble lodging *chez Madame Papillote, rez-de-chaussée.* But rumours are not invariably correct, and therefore we are not bound to believe that mademoiselle, if she falls, will not be the first victim of her sex by many who have perished in swamps, attracted thither by the will-o'-the-wisp of his wonderful beauty; nor that he once caused a disobedient servant to be tortured to death; nor that—but why recall them all? They are doubtless exaggerated, for even in distant Hungary—he is a Hungarian—there must, *même pour les princes,* be something like law.

'Yet there is one crime laid to his charge

of so serious a nature, that I cannot refrain from mentioning it. He was not always the ruling prince. There was an elder brother whom the people loved, for he was brave and good and gentle, and this brother died—was killed. Let me tell you how.

'One day there was to be a grand boar hunt in the forest, and the princes, both of whom were passionately fond of this diversion, were to take part in it. I heard from a by-stander, one of the suite, that it was a splendid sight to see them mounted, a gallant retinue surrounding them, the bugles blowing, the hounds straining at their leashes and panting for the chase. The princess mother—step-mother of the elder, and who hated him—was there to see them depart, and it was remembered long after how the elder prince turned back towards her, his impatient horse rearing high at the sudden check, to say, "Mother, there is a strange foreboding in my heart; if

I have ever sinned against thee, forgive it now, for the sake of this my brother, whom we both love so dearly."

'The people never forgot how the pale cheek of the princess turned to sickly yellow at these noble words, nor how she shrank from him as if his soft voice had been a blow. They remembered too how the younger prince—Prince Eberhard—struck his spurs into the flanks of the fiery animal he rode, so that it started off at a fierce gallop. The whole brilliant cavalcade followed, leaving behind in the courtyard of the palace a silence like the silence of death.

'Never was such a hunt. Every shot told, and the princes and their followers seemed alike insatiable. At last the day began to fade, and they were forced to return to the spot where the horses were waiting.

'As they turned to go, another shot

echoed through the darkening wood, followed
by a cry of such intense horror that every
leaflet in the broad forest, every startled bird
in the thickets, every drop of blood in the
hearts present seemed to stand still to listen.
And then the people knew that the noblest
of them all had fallen—that it was the life-
blood of their beloved prince which was
sickening every blade of grass upon the
sward. After this manner your enemy and
mine, monsieur, came into the rights of the
firstborn.

'Yet the people said it was an accident.'

My little friend at this point sank into
reflection—reflection which was so deep and
profound that he only emerged from it at the
gates of Lucerne.

'Behold our destination,' he cried, 'and
my story is only just begun.'

'Finish,' I said. 'Let us turn again ; my
time is my own.'

'But not mine,' he answered, shrugging his shoulders, and looking up at me with his expressive French grimace. 'What a delusion it is of ours, my friend, to think we rule the women, when, nine times out of ten, they so despotically rule us.'

'What has that to do with your story?'

'Only this, that it terminates it for the present. I shall get something warm for supper to-night, and yet go to bed hungry and cold. There's a riddle for you.'

'Come to my hotel and sup with me.'

'*Merci bien, mon ami*, but I prefer to pay to-day's debts to-day. *Au revoir.*'

'Come and breakfast with me to-morrow.'

'I will do that gladly, and finish my story too, if it will not weary you.'

And he was gone, first having saluted military fashion, his open hand against his shabby hat. There was something military in his walk too, I thought, as I watched him pacing down the street from under the broad *porte-cochère* of my hotel.

Well, Fate had poured a good deal into my empty life this day!

CHAPTER IX.

A CÔTELETTE, A CAT, AND A CAPTAIN.

L'homme est si grand que sa grandeur paroit même en ce
qu'il se connoit misérable. Un arbre ne se connoit pas misérable.
Il est vrai que c'est être misérable que de se connoître misérable ; mais c'est aussi être grand que de connoître qu'on est
misérable. Ainsi toutes ces misères prouvent sa grandeur. Ce
sont misères de grand seigneur, misères d'un roi détrôné.

PASCAL.

I WAS long in sinking to sleep, and when I
awoke it was hardly yet morning. I walked
to my window, threw it open, and looked out.

Long rows of lighted windows casting
faint reflections on the lake showed me that
the ever-active *Kellner* were at their morning
work, and Nature outside was astir and busy
trimming the mighty lamp which would soon
extinguish the others every one. The east

was bright in glowing expectation of the returning monarch of day; the usurping moon had fled in alarm; the stars, his courtiers, were wan and pale in the morning sky; the mountains were shaking off the mists in which their heads had been shrouded during the night; the green waters of the lake were rippling a musical welcome to the golden sunbeams; while the snowy top of many a virgin peak was beginning to crimson like the pure cheek of a maiden under the fiery kiss of her lover.

I had been restless during the night, haunted by many strange visions. Little white dogs, clammy with blood, had looked up at me with human eyes, and spoken to me with human voices. Beauteous ladies had called upon me to come to their assistance. Frenchmen had rescued me from poisonous daggers levelled at my heart, and, oddly enough, the instant afterwards challenged me

to mortal combat.   Gendarmes had dragged
me off to prison, to die there at my leisure,
like the fair lady of Ballyacora Hall. Madame
Papillote had snatched untasted suppers from
my famishing lips.   Princes had fallen before
me like stubble before the wind.   And in the
midst of all I had felt Aileen's wet cheek
against my own, while my father stood up to
curse me, only prevented by a woman's
resolute hand over his mouth, and a woman's
earnest voice saying, 'Let the cruel thing
that weaned a brother from a sister answer
that.'

The full day had been succeeded by a
fuller night. A thousand interests had sprung
up in a life which had been atrophising for
want of one.

My new leader was as punctual as the
waiter with our breakfast, and the last stroke
of ten found us together in the private room
where I had ordered it should be laid. I

would not let him talk much until his
appetite was appeased, for I had noted the
wistful glance he cast upon the viands, and
remembered his own sombre prediction of
the night before.

So I replenished his plate with every good
thing I could find to put upon it, keenly
watching him while I ostensibly played with
my knife and fork, for I had no appetite,
because I believe you may gain much knowledge of a man's character from the way in
which he eats. And as I watched, my confidence in him was confirmed, and my heart
went out to this new acquaintance freely and
unreservedly.

For, firstly, he ate like a gentleman ; he
was undeniably hungry, and the viands were
such as to give the spur to appetite, but in
the midst of his appreciation and enjoyment
he never forgot propriety. Then, again, he
ate like a man of sound and unimpaired

digestion.   Beginning with more substantial
dainties, he finished up with a huge slice of
sweet cake—which I couldn't have touched—
and finally pledged me in a glass of sparkling
Veuve Clicquot, his eyes as sparkling as it,
like a man who knows the use but not the
abuse of the good gifts of God.   Your drunkard cannot eat like that, still less the man of
vicious life.   I was only twenty-two, and he
at least, sixty; but, alas! I couldn't remember
the meal which had given me half the innocent pleasure.

'Behold me   satisfied   at last,' he said.
'Truly, monsieur, you have entertained me
with a *déjeuner* fit for a prince.'

'Did you get any supper last night?' I
asked, smiling.

'Ah, you may well inquire, judging of
my prowess to-day! No, monsieur, but the
cat did.'

'The cat?'

'Monsieur, she is an animal of great discernment. She acts as my Nemesis.'

'Why don't you hang her?'

'Sooth to say, monsieur, such a thought has sometimes come to me, but I have rejected it. Do not we prey upon all animals? Can we blame them if they sometimes prey upon us? Nevertheless I think that my Nemesis is sometimes hard upon me.'

'How?'

'A little punishment is salutary, monsieur, and teaches us humility, but an overdose is a folly as well as a wrong, because it rouses up resistance. Now I confess to having felt badly treated this morning when my coffee and *petit pain* also were appropriated by that insatiable animal. And I could not quite agree with Madame Papillote, who said that I deserved it.'

I laughed. There was something comical

in his distress, and in the droll way in which
he gave it utterance.

'Ah, monsieur, you laugh and Madame
Papillote scolds, yet for all that I find that
my little cross is sometimes hard to bear.
Madame Papillote says she is a mother to
me, but, to tell the truth, I feel occasionally
that she is more *marâtre* than *mère*. However, we have had enough of myself. Let us
consider what to do next. And, firstly, can
you still, after a night's rest, consent with all
your heart to be my ally?'

'To be your *aide de camp*, to follow your
banner? Yes, monsieur, with all my heart.'

'And you do not even first inquire who
I am?'

'No, monsieur. Your face is in the full
light of day, and there is no shadow there to
shame it. Your eyes meet mine straight and
unflinchingly. For the rest, I have heard you
talk and I have seen you eat.'

It was his turn to laugh now, and he did laugh heartily. But there was something like a mist before his eyes, and his hand trembled as he put it into his pocket.

'You gave me a grand testimony yesterday, *mon ami*, and you gave it me unsolicited and with frank confidence. You said I was a gentleman, and you did not mean that I was an aristocrat, did you?'

I checked the smile which began to curl my lips as my eye rested involuntarily on his well-brushed pantaloons, his frayed linen collar and shiny surtout, and I answered boldly, 'I did not.'

'*Merci bien, monsieur.* Thank you heartily for that as well as for the other. I have a little word to say to you about the aristocrats before we commence our work. *Un tout petit mot, monsieur;* do not have fear. In the meantime, *regardez.*'

He had drawn a card from his pocket,

carefully wrapped in a scrap of newspaper.
I opened it and read:

LOUIS-ADOLPHE MOPPERT,

Capitaine au 67ᵐᵉ Régiment de Ligne.

'Ha, a soldier! A real captain to fight
under!'

'I *was* a soldier, monsieur. I helped, side
by side with many a brave comrade, to fight
a grand battle for France. But we did not
risk our lives and the lives of those dear to
us—we other Frenchmen—to grovel at the
feet of an emperor. We did not drive out
kings and their sycophants to worship a
golden calf in the shape of a Napoleon. Bear
witness, all ye other nations of the earth, we
were not fools enough for that!'

He had sprung to his feet, his fist clenched,
his mild, sometimes sarcastic, eye irate and
fiery.

'Pardon, monsieur,' he added more
quietly, as he reseated himself, 'it is a subject

which puts every drop of my old blood into
motion, and makes me twenty-six again instead
of sixty. For they offered me—*me*, monsieur—
a *de* before my honest name—they would have
made of me—of Moppert, monsieur—a hatch-
ing duke ! '

'And you would rather be yourself?'

'In my humble lodging, *rez-de-chaussée*,
chez Madame Papillote—a cat the arbiter of
my destiny. *Mais oui, monsieur*, you have
said it.'

I was silent and sat watching him, my
head upon my hand.

'My face is in the full light, as you have
already remarked, monsieur, and yours, facing
it, is therefore in shadow, and still further
shrouded by your hand. I feel the expression
you partially hide rather than see it, and I
feel it in my inmost soul.'

'What expression, monsieur?'

'Listen, *mon ami;* speak truth to Moppert,

even if that truth must murder remorselessly
a new-born hope. Let it perish rather than
be reared upon a lie.'

'What is it you want to know, monsieur?
Ask, and I will answer like—like an honest
man.'

'*Bon!* that is better even than gentleman.
Tell me then, would you have consented more
willingly to work with me if I had been a
duke, or even Monsieur *de* Moppert?'

'Not one iota.'

'*Bon* again! My soul begins to expand.
I shake off one fear which was heavy upon it.'

'Yet another remains?'

'Truly, monsieur, I will be as honest as
you and frankly avow it. There *is* another.
It has shrunk to half its size, but is not dead.
It breathes, it moves, it is capable of growth
still.'

'Tell it me.'

'I will go back a little way and tell you

how it was begotten. It had no existence
yesterday. And first I will tell you how it
was that I ventured to speak to you yesterday,
and even to act for you, the stranger. I was
on my quest as usual. I was looking for an
ally. You are not the first whom Monsieur
de Pöbeldowski has wantonly insulted. He
takes deliberate pleasure in forcing everyone
with whom he comes in contact to lick the
dust. And there are many, monsieur, who
feel it an honour to lick dust at the feet of a
prince.

'But even before that thunderous en-
counter, when for the first time he met with
furious opposition, I had been watching you
with interest. You are young, handsome,
evidently rich. Why should *you* have stood
among the gay crowd like an image of despair ?
—no, not of despair, you had left that behind,
and there was nothing beyond you but death.'

I started. By what magical power had

the little man been enabled to look into my heart?

'Yet at the very moment when you thought you had outlived love, love was close beside you, waiting to lay a thrilling touch upon your heart. The very power to hate had perished within you, you fancied, when all the time hate was sharpening a dagger to put into your hand. You deemed that you had done with life, when life roughly came to shake you out of your lethargy, saying, "It is work, not pleasure, which is my aim and end. I have work for thee to do ; come and do it !"'

It was true. I had learned to live anew since yesterday.

'A few minutes later, monsieur, I knew that I had found my ally, and that the ally was one after my own heart. For it is when the passions are all ablaze that we see the man as he is. There is no concealing crust of conventionality over him then. Yesterday I thought you were *bourgeois* like myself.'

' And to-day, monsieur?'

' To-day I am puzzled, anxious, and uneasy. You have very much the air of a *grand seigneur* as you sit there before me, and a *grand seigneur* is to me what a cat is to a dog. Nature makes me want to worry him. I do not like that curl on your lip, nor those beringed hands, nor that *insouciant* smile, which seems as natural to you as the *fauteuil* on which you are lounging. Look at *my* hands; and as for *fauteuils*, monsieur, a wooden stool is the seat for which *I* was born!'

' Well, suppose I am an aristocrat?'

' *Je m'en doute, monsieur.* You are either one, or have lived so much among them that you have imbibed a good deal of—let us say their odour. Well, I accept the inevitable. I will not let my dislike for a class lead me

into injustice against an individual. Give me
the hand, monsieur. We will be allies and—
and friends all the same.'

'Or suppose I am not?'

'Ah, monsieur, you must not mock yourself of Moppert. I—I accept the inevitable,
but I cannot joke about it. I have suffered
too much, I and France, to bear even a light
finger on that wound. I am a republican to
the nails on my fingers and toes, monsieur.
I may love you, but I cannot love your class.
I cannot lift a hand to save—nay, I am compelled to help to drive them to their certain
doom. *Bon Dieu!* Were the millions made
for the few, or the few for the millions?'

'Be consoled, monsieur. I am no more an
aristocrat than yourself. I am nothing and
nobody.'

And I covered my face with my hands,
ashamed of my useless life and the years I had
wasted.

He almost sprang to the ceiling in his excitement. He clasped me to his heart, embracing me again and again.

'*Venez*,' he cried. 'Even this big salon is too small to hold me. Let us go down to the lake and smoke a cigarette, and lay our plans with clearer heads than we have now. Come, my friend.'

I instantly acceded to his proposal, and we passed out of the shadow of the salon into the brilliant sunshine of the glowing noon outside.

CHAPTER X.

JOSEF AUFDERMAUER.

Auf den Bergen wohnt die Freiheit, und am Meere wird
man niemals Sclave.—GUTZKOW.

THERE was not a cloud to be seen in the deep
blue of the sky as we passed out from under
the shadow of the broad *porte-cochère*, and the
rugged summit of Mount Pilate stood out
darkly distinct from its brilliant sapphire
background.   As we sauntered down to the
water's edge, lazily puffing the smoke from
our scented cigarettes, I was struck by the
extreme stillness of the emerald water and the
unwonted richness of its colouring.   Everything seemed sunk in repose except ourselves ;
the very flies had ceased to buzz over the

glassy surface of the water, unharassed by
the fish which lay motionless under them, and
the houses of Lucerne, their windows hidden
behind green venetian blinds, were slumber-
ing with their inmates. The sun, high in the
heavens, sent scorching rays down upon the
burning earth, which, like a heated stove,
seemed to give back what it received with
usury. The only moving things were a
solitary pleasure-boat, lazily propelled by the
hands of some doubtlessly mad Englishman,
and the smoke from a steamer bound for
Flüelen, which, too weary to rise, fell darkly
back upon its deck again.

'*Comme il fait chaud!*' said Moppert.

'How hot it is!' I repeated.

'It was cooler yonder in the *salon,*' said
my little friend, lighting a fresh cigarette.
'We had better have stayed there, *mon ami.*
Look how intensely blue the sky is, and how
clearly defined the peaks of Mount Pilate ; yet

I never remember this burning, sulphurous feel
in the air since the night I found Gracieuse.
And that was followed by a fearful storm,
though there is no sign of a storm to-day.'

'Not one,' I answered, untying my cravat
and loosening my collar. 'It was certainly
cooler in the *salon*, as you say ; nevertheless, I
do not want to go back.'

'Youth never does,' said the Frenchman
quietly ; 'it leaves that for age.'

'Look at the boat yonder,' I said ; 'the
Spaniards say that only dogs and Englishmen
go abroad in the sunshine of the noon-day,
but you may depend upon it the rower is
right. If there is a breath of air to be found
anywhere it will be upon the lake.'

'*Me voilà tout prêt*,' said Moppert, 'and
there are boats enough ; but where is the
boatman ?'

I looked round. There were plenty of
boats, big ones and little ones ; some drawn

up upon the shore, some upon the water; but
not a single man to be seen anywhere, only a
barefooted boy, sitting under the shadow of a
boat, nursing a baby.

'See, there's little Josef,' said Moppert.
'How is the baby, Josef?'

'Pretty quiet just now, sir, thank you.'

'That little lad is the eldest of seven,' said
Moppert. 'We call him the boy-mother, because his mother is bedridden, and he takes
care of the others. Poor little lad, he is a
cripple.'

I drew out a piece of gold.

The boy's eyes glistened, but he put out
no hand to receive it.

'Herre, I have done nothing to earn it.'

'But you shall,' I said; 'fetch me a boatman.'

'Fetch your father, Josef,' said Moppert;
'he is the best boatman in Lucerne; and take
the money for the mother.'

The boy took it now, though with much
hesitation. ' The mother is ill,' he said, the
colour rushing to his face. Then he limped
off, baby and all.

' When I have had a particularly hard
time with Madame Papillote and her cat,' said
the Frenchman gravely, ' I come down to
the shore and let that cripple lad teach me
how to bear. He will not teach for long,
monsieur. Such as he die early.'

A moment more of waiting and then
Moppert cried :

' *Voici* Josef's father ! Good-day, Aufdermauer.'

The man touched his cap in acknowledg-
ment of the greeting.

' Good-day, gentlemen,' he responded.
' Was it you who sent our Josef to request me
to find you a boat ? '

His use of the word ' request ' (*bitten*) instead
of ' command,' the free-and-easy manner of his

salutation, courteous, but with the courtesy of
a lieutenant to his colonel—gentlemen both—
impressed me. And I thought of William
Tell, and wondered if he in any way resembled
this man.

'Yes,' I said, 'we want a boat; find us
one as soon as possible.'

He did not speak for a moment, only
turned his dark eyes up towards the sky, letting
them rest on the summit of Mount Pilate.

'Mount Pilate has no collar on to-day,'
said Moppert. 'I know the signs of the
weather as well as you, Aufdermauer. To-
day a child might row on *Vierwaldstätter-See.*'

'Gentlemen,' said the boatman, without
replying to this remark, 'my boat will be
ready in five minutes; it is lying yonder. I
will row you myself.'

'We do not want a boatman,' I said; 'I
shall not require you.'

'Gentlemen,' said the boatman again, after

another rapid glance at sky and lake, 'I will take you out for a row myself and be glad to do it. I was born here on the shores of the lake and know what Mount Pilate means when he lifts a finger. You must not go out alone to-day.'

Must not? I had been one of the crack rowers at Oxford, and this man's evident contempt for my prowess nettled me. I was a spoiled child of fortune, and his ' must not ' made me determined that I would.

' Get your boat ready,' I repeated haughtily. ' We shall not want you.'

His dark eyes flashed, then he said with effort : 'Sir, I have seen the piece of gold you gave our Josef, and I cannot take it away from my wife again, who has already shed tears of joy over it. Hear me a moment. Last summer, a young man, one of your countrymen, took his bride out alone upon the lake.'

'What has that to do with me?'

'Only this, Herre,' he continued, his great dark eyes flashing again; 'only this, that the young wife sleeps now in the churchyard of Lucerne, and he, the harebrained husband, sleeps, and wakes, both in a madhouse. You cannot turn a deaf ear to the spirits of our lakes; they will be heeded and obeyed.'

I was staggered. For a moment I thought of yielding, then I raised my eyes to the sky and laughed at the absurdity of his fear. There was not a cloud in it as big as a man's hand. The boatman was only humbugging us in order to increase the value of his services.

'I am poor,' continued the man—an obvious fact of which he did not need to inform us—'and can make use of every centime I earn, but I would rather not earn another franc this week than let you go out alone to-day.'

Let us, forsooth! Who was this man that
he dared gainsay my wishes? The idle desire
of half an hour ago had grown into a furious
longing under the stimulus of opposition.

'If you cannot supply us with a boat,
there are others who can, I suppose,' I said with
simulated coolness. 'For the rest, there was
no need of your putting so much stress on
your value. I should have paid you as much
for your absence as for your presence.'

The man's strong frame quivered with
suppressed passion. 'Sir, it is not that,' he
said ; 'you know it is not that. I am paid
already. There is my boat, it is unmoored,
take it. The dear God knows I have done
what I could.'

In another minute or so we were in the
boat, a rapidly increasing space of green
water between it and the handsome figure of
Josef Aufdermauer, who stood looking after
us, his hand shading his eyes from the burn-

ing sunlight. I had heard his parting words to Moppert, who had followed me mechanically. 'Herre,' he said, 'you are older and wiser than the *Engländer*; for heaven's sake, keep your eye upon Mount Pilate.'

I pulled hard at the oars in spite of the heat, ashamed to look at my friend, who sat motionless by the rudder and uttered not a word. I knew, too, that I lied when I said, a few minutes later:

' *Ce ne sont que des sottises, monsieur.* The fellow wanted to humbug us.'

'You have said it,' he answered monotonously, using his customary words of assent, but with no assent in them now. 'But how hot it is—how hot it is!'

It *was* hot for a certainty. The sweat stood in thick beads upon my forehead. There was a suffocating feel in the air, which compelled us to draw our breath with effort, or hold it with nature. The blue vault,

arched so high above, nevertheless weighed
upon us like an incubus, and the smoke from
the chimneys in Lucerne, like the smoke of
the steamer, too sluggish to rise, fell back
again upon the city. I would have returned
but for shame, and I resolved to keep a strict
watch, and to pull for the shore on the
slightest sign of disturbance in the sky. In
the meantime I must arouse Moppert, and induce him to look at me, instead of at Mount
Pilate.

'Tell me the rest of your story,' I said;
'I can row and listen too.'

My ruse was successful. His face brightened. His anxious eye cleared. He turned
his head away from the shore, and the two
bugbears there, the mountain and the mountain's interpreter, and looked at me instead.

I put into my face a confidence I did not
feel. I smiled his fears away, and rowing hard,

in order to lose sight of Josef Aufdermauer, encouraged him to begin.

We were now alone upon the lake. The solitary boat with its occupant had disappeared, and the quiet around us was undisturbed except by the splash of my oars. Moppert began to narrate, and soon, in the interest of his story, which made the beads on his forehead swell into heavy drops and fall, we had both forgotten Josef Aufdermauer, and his warning to keep an eye upon Mount Pilate.

CHAPTER XI.

THE REASON WHY.

Et via vix tandem voci laxata dolore est.—VIRGIL (*Æneid*).
Chi può dir com' egli arde, è un picciol fuoco.—PETRARCA.

'THE little dog did not die, monsieur. I washed the blood from its wounds, put it in the bed beside me, and let it lie there until the morning.

'Whether it slept or not, I cannot tell. The storm which Mount Pilate had announced broke upon us, and during it sleep was impossible for me. My little room was illuminated by a light more intense than that of the sun to-day, and the crash of the thunder was so terrible and continuous, that more than

once I thought Lucerne must have fallen, as
did the walls of Jericho.

'When it subsided, I arose from my sleepless couch, and looked long at my unique
bed-fellow.

'It was not sleeping then. It was gazing
up at me with dark, soft, trustful eyes, for all
the world like those of my lost Gracieuse.

'Then I stooped and took it in my arms
and said: "See, little one! Thou and I art
outcasts: both of us have been cruelly ill-
used by those whom we would have loved
and honoured. Let us live henceforth together, foregoing the vengeance I have sworn
during this night. Didst thou, too, understand the words of the thunder when it said:
' Vengeance is Mine?'"

'It wagged its tail, monsieur, just as if it
had, and licked my hand ; and so we sealed
our compact, Gracieuse and I, and the dog
became my own.

'We led a harassed life though, for the next week or two. Madame Papillote extorted a most exorbitant price for its board, putting me also upon short rations to make up for it in another way. As for the cat —monsieur, I confess—there is yet a little bottle of poison in my cupboard, hidden behind the tisane, and a bit of rope.

'We could not stand it at last. I was obliged to seek other lodgings for Gracieuse. So I took her to the hut of a charcoal-burner, and left her there in charge of the man's blind daughter, Gabrielle. I was forced to hide her for fear of her meeting her former master and would-be murderer; but every day, weather permitting, I took my promenade in the wood, spending my happiest hours there with Gracieuse, both of us what the Germans call *vogelfrei*.

'I must not forget to say that I sent back the blue leather collar, its costly gold em-

broidery all stained with blood, to Monsieur
le prince. And I added a few lines written
in blood too—the blood of the dog. They
were but a few: only to the effect that, if we
ever came into contact, it should be his fault ;
but *if* we did, Heaven have mercy on him, for
I would have none.

'How much I learned to love the dog,
monsieur, I hardly venture to tell you. You
would think it folly, no doubt. But the pretty
creature loved me, and seemed to know that
it was I who had saved it. It would run from
Gabrielle to meet me, frantic with delight, and
on those days that I could not come, it would
refuse its food, sitting with drooping tail and
ears in a corner, an image of desolation.

'Thus the months slipped by and the
golden leaves turned to russet brown, and,
dropping one by one, were covering the earth
with a brown mantle to protect it from the
winter's cold.

' I noticed this as I walked through the wood towards the hut, by the side of a little rippling rivulet imbedded in a stony couch softened by moss. No bird was singing, but my heart supplied the deficiency, and sang a duet with the water, as it murmured of the clear lake towards which it was hastening. My heart felt unusually blithe that day; the air was fresh though soft, permeated by that peculiarly invigorating element which only autumn yields.

' Monsieur, if you are not tired, row a little harder for a moment, that my nerves may be steadied by the feeling of *doing* something. Did you ever feel particularly well just before an illness, or particularly happy just when Fate was raising the knife to cut the throat of your happiness?

' I was surprised to find the cottage door close shut: it was usually wide open to welcome me. And why was Gracieuse so tardy?

and what had silenced Gabrielle's clear song ?
Yet I smiled ; I smiled, monsieur, as I tapped
at the door. Ha! ha! the soft wind had
carried away the sound of my coming ; they
were not expecting me, and all the greater
would be their delight.

'My rap was answered, but—by what ?
By the piteous, terrified, imploring howl of a
dog ! Then silence so profound that the gentle
ripple of the rivulet sounded like the roar of
a cataract.

'I tried the door : it was fastened.

'I knocked again ; loudly, angrily, imperatively. My heart's rapid beat sounded as
ominous as the tick of the death-watch, and the
sweat stood on my brow in thicker drops than
it does to-day. Was that fierce, harsh voice
mine, saying : " *Gracieuse, ma petite, sois tranquille ! C'est moi.*"

'The next moment I was in the one room
of the cottage ; half of it stove, on the top of

which poor blind Gabrielle slept. Gabrielle
was not there ; only Gracieuse, crouched in a
corner, her bright eyes wide with terror.

'Monsieur, row a little faster still, if you
please. I *must* feel like *doing something* while
I speak. Oh, the pain, the pain of this inaction ! the torture of being forced to *wait*
instead of fight !

'I suppose I had broken open the door
myself. I cannot tell. I only know that I
was there, as I should have been if stone walls
had tried to shut me out. There are crises in
our lives, monsieur, when we can do *anything*,
when every earthly consideration, every conventional bond, nay, even apparently insuper-
able obstacles, are as powerless to restrain us
as the thread of a spider's web.

'There were two or three men in the room.
I *felt* their presence, for my eyes saw nothing
but Gracieuse. I knew, too, who they were ;
for, monsieur, if we are warned instinctively

of the nearness of what we love, we feel still
more infallibly the contact of what we hate.

'But I spoke quietly—oh, so quietly!—
raising my hat and bowing low as I said:
" Gentlemen, pardon my intrusion; I am
gone again in a moment. It is but to fetch
my dog that I come." And I added, more
softly still: " *Gracieuse, ma petite, sois tranquille! C'est moi.*"

'I stooped and took her in my arms,
monsieur, and the trance of terror into which
she had fallen dispersed somewhat when she
felt my caress. I stroked her silky hair and
pressed her to my heart, turning to go without another word — as noiselessly, as sub-
missively as if I had been an unhallowed
intruder into a sanctuary and these men its
high priests. When I passed their chief, I
bowed low again and entreatingly, as if
beseeching him to forgive my sacrilege.
For oh, monsieur, love is very powerful;

it can teach us to bear profoundest humiliation, forcing us even to lick the dust from the feet of a Prince de Pöbeldowski!

'I had only taken a few steps, when a voice, as quiet as mine, called on me to stop. You have heard its liquid music, monsieur. Could Satan, tempting Christ in the wilderness, have found a voice better suited for his purpose than that?

' " By what right are you its master? " said the prince.

'I turned and looked straight into the face I hated so intensely. I saw the triumphant sparkle in his eye, the quivering of his nostril, the smile curling his lips—like the smile of a tiger ready to spring. And I forgot my humanity as I looked, in the brutish instinct to fly at his throat and cling there, until he, or I, or both of us, were dead.'

I had been rowing almost as rapidly as

the Frenchman had been narrating—the high
tension of feeling into which he had worked
us both passing on into my muscles until
I grew insensible to fatigue. Now, as he
paused, I paused also, resting on my oars
and letting the boat drive with the current.
We had long since lost sight of Lucerne.

' " By what right ? " said the prince.

' " By a right divine and sacred," I
answered—and now my voice was choked
with passion and tremulous with fury—" the
right of having saved it from a cruel death."

' " A very poetical right, truly," laughed
the prince—his companions laughing with
him—" but hardly a legal one, monsieur. I
bought and paid for the dog, and *my* right,
though psychologically less interesting than
yours, is more likely to be regarded. But I
have no time to refer the matter to others.
I am already *en route* for Hungary. I must
settle it at once."

'In spite of the sneer in his tone, his words seemed to point out a hope. In spite of the cruel gleam in his eye, I seized the hope and clung to it.

'"Let me buy the dog," I cried eagerly. "I am poor, but I will borrow money. I will work, I will starve, to pay the price you name."

'"The dog is priceless," he answered, "there is not its fellow in Europe. You might sell yourself and fail to realise its value. But for lack of time, I would have you arrested for dog-stealing."

'"Monsieur," I answered, "have a care. I am a soldier of France."

'"So much the better," he replied, "we will settle it on the spot. It was you, therefore, who sent me back the collar and the words accompanying it."

'"Monsieur," I said beseechingly (do not think meanly of me, my friend, it was for

Gracieuse) " those words were written in hot anger : forget them, as I will."

' " I never forget," he answered, " and never forgive. Those words were written in blood ; I shall give them back in blood, to-day."

' I trembled. Monsieur, I am not afraid to die. I have stood firm at the cannon's mouth and rushed forward upon fixed bayonets with a cry of delight, but now I turned sick with fear. There was something impending over me I should not be able to bear.

' " I make a proposition to you, monsieur,' continued the prince. " Look at the dog, she knows me better than you do ; she knows that I never forgive."

' It was true. Her fear of him, *pauvre petite*, was greater than her confidence in me. She had sprung from my arms and was lying crouched at his feet—not in hope of averting her doom : oh, my God! not in hope !

' " She used to be my favourite," he went on, smiling that cruel smile of his, " and she ventured to disobey me. I punished her. Look here."

'He opened his beautiful right hand and showed me the palm. There was a slight scar upon it.

' " She ventured further to resent her punishment, monsieur, and then——well, you know what then."

'Yes, I knew, I knew ! But, like a prudent soldier, I spared my forces until every tittle of them would be needed for action.

' " I spoke of a proposition, monsieur," continued the prince. " If you accede to it, I will make you a free gift of Donna, unharmed."

'There was no sign of hope in his words now, not a particle. I waited.

'"I have been seeking you and Donna, monsieur, many a long day," he said. "I had nearly given you up in despair. But fortune favoured me : she always does."

'I waited still.

'This morning—only this morning—one of my people recognised Donna with a blind girl on the outskirts of Lucerne."

'Oh, unhappy Gabrielle! How wilt thou bear to hear what thou hast done?

'"Only blood will satisfy me," he continued ; "yours or the dog's. I will accept a propitiatory sacrifice. Once she was my favourite. I liked to feel her lick my hand and rub her head against my knee."

'Oh, great God, are there not chords even in this man's heart which may be touched to tenderness! Oh, blessed and pitiful Virgin, he had once a mother and Thou a son!

'"I give you your choice," he continued. "Bare your back to my executioner ; we will

only flog you to within an inch of your life;
and Donna shall be yours." And he added:
" Do *you* like to have her lick your hand and
rub her head against your knee ? "

' Only think of this, *mon ami*—of this to
me, a soldier of France !

' " I cast your infamous proposition back
in your teeth ! " I cried ; and now I rushed
upon him, ready to struggle to the death. " I
am a soldier and an officer : my honour is
dearer to me than my life."

' " You have chosen," he answered, and as
he spoke I was seized by his vile companions,
who held me as in a vice.

' Monsieur, I was one and they were two ;
I was old and comparatively feeble, they were
young and vigorous ; yet twice I wrenched
my pinioned arms loose ere I was conquered.

' It was *he* who struck her—*he*, who had
once loved to feel her lick his hand and rub
her soft head against his knee ! When I saw

the red blood spout from the wound, my spirit succumbed as well as my body; my love was stronger than my honour. I cried out: "Do with me as you will, but spare her!"

'I yielded in vain, monsieur. He only struck again, laughing and saying: "You have chosen, and I know now which punishment is the greater."

'She was not long in dying. The first blow, or the terror of it, stunned her on the spot, for she uttered no further sound. When he paused and they liberated me, we all stood still a moment—the murderers as well as I—with bated breath and paling faces, for something terrible seemed to rise up from the spot, red with her life-blood, and to stand there in the midst of us.

'No one spoke a word when I lifted her and pressed her to my heart. No one sought to hinder me. I passed unmolested through

the midst of them, opened the door of the
cottage, and stepped out into the porch.

'There I turned, quite tearless and com-
posed, and said quietly—more quietly than
ever—for God was speaking, and all creation
holding its breath to listen :

' " Prince, we shall meet again, and it will
be my turn then. Look—and I raised the
dog high—look at the debt you have incurred,
and remember that it must all be paid to the
uttermost farthing."

'I buried her, monsieur, in a little dell
in the forest, where, over her grave, violets
would spring and birds warble. But I shed
no tear over the spot, nor uttered one moan,
nor chanted one requiem. The heavier a
blow is the more it stuns, and feeling at its
intensest is as silent as the tomb.

'Only a dog, monsieur, only a dog, and
yet God knows——!'

As he ceased, plucking fiercely at his

moustache, I heard a deep sigh float towards us over the water, and a muttered sound, which seemed to issue from the base of the mountains. The air was agitated and two or three huge fish leaped suddenly, close to the boat's prow. I looked up to the sky and saw that its blue was beflecked by many a flying cloud, all hastening towards the sun, now strongly inclining towards the west. 'Monsieur,' I cried, 'we have forgotten the boatman's warning. I cannot see Mount Pilate, but is it not a certain sign of a storm when the fish are so restless? Had I not better pull for the shore?'

CHAPTER XII.

THE FÖHN.

O solve me the riddle of human life,
The riddle as terrible as it is old,——
Tell me what is the meaning of man?
Whence doth he come? and for where is he bound?
Translated from HEINE.

I HAD hardly uttered these words before the
air was darkened and the sun as completely
hidden as if he had already sunk behind
the mountains. Huge masses of cloud covered
the sky, which had turned to an indescrib-
able colour. It was neither purple nor red,
but looked as if it were illuminated by
some gigantic and infernal firework shining
through a dense veil of mist. And it spread
and spread, until not only the firmament, but

also the surrounding mountains and the water itself, might have been nothing more tangible than the smoke of hell's own fire.

And in the midst of this our boat stood still—struck motionless; wrapt round with a brightly gleaming pall.

We not only felt the lurid death all around us, but we smelt and tasted it too. Upon our heads, upon our hands, upon our lungs, it weighed with crushing power. It was not so much the water that we feared ; it was the air.

Nature was dumb, and with a menacing finger on our lips struck us dumb too.

I tried my utmost to break the awful charm, but only a feeble sigh issued from my loaded breast.

As if even this faint sound had subdued the spell, something unseen and terrible, perhaps the spirit of the lake, sighed a deep echo. A large fish sprang so high and close to me, that the water it disturbed splashed my face. The air became violently agitated, and a deep bell rang out a solemn warning from the shore. A phantom sound, ringing out our knell.

I looked at Moppert. With wide, dilated eyes he looked back at me.

Then, with a gasp, my voice came back to me. 'Good God!' I cried, 'tell me what to do!' I instinctively felt that man's help would be in vain.

'*Mon ami*,' said Moppert in a voice as hoarse and hopeless as the croak of a raven, 'do you know what that bell is saying?'

I could not answer him. I clutched the oars again. If I had to die, I would die fighting.

'It is the herald of the Föhn,' continued Moppert. 'It is to tell the people to put out their fires and candles and to pray for the souls of those upon the lake.'

For their *souls* only, and I was yet so young, so young !

I saw Moppert, with the lurid light upon his pallid face, looking round wildly as if to find some ray of hope in any one point of the compass. I saw him cross himself, and clasp his hands and bow his head, at finding none.

'Let us pray,' he said. 'Catholic or Protestant, there is but one God, and He is almighty.'

I was still so young, so young ! I would break that sombre curtain and die, at least, in the open. I would not be pent up in a grave while yet alive.

I pulled at the oars. The boat moved again.

I pulled at the oars till they bent in my hands. We were probably rushing upon death ; but anything was better than to sit still in hopeless waiting.

In the meantime the sighs from the unseen

spirit had increased in volume and intensity, until at last they rose to piercing shrieks, which might have been uttered under the agony of some infernal rack, beyond even the power of a spirit to endure. And now the placid water began to shudder, and to rock us as fiercely upon her bosom as an angry nurse might rock an unruly child.

The lurid light had faded, and the darkness grew so intense that I could no longer see Moppert. The horror of being quite alone in the midst of this awful exhibition of God's power was too great to be endured, and I cried out to him to come to me.

He came at once, creeping along the bottom of the boat, until his hand touched my knee and his warm breath was on my cheek. And we clung together, comforted even in this crisis by that human sympathy which is the most precious thing God has given us, and which can help us even in the agony of death.

'Forgive me,' I said; 'forgive the wicked obstinacy which refused to heed honest warning, and which has cost us both our lives.'

'Forgive *me*,' he answered; 'I was older, and ought to have been wiser.'

Alas! he spoke in the past tense already.

Then the black pall shrouding earth and heaven was rent asunder for a moment by a flaming sword of fire. I saw his face again once more and he saw mine.

He was looking his fate full in her terrible eyes with the calm, resigned look of a soldier and a hero. He was not afraid to die. Yet when we embraced, my first and last passionate prayer went up to God to save him, and let me alone bear the punishment.

The vivid light had hardly been succeeded by darkness which might be felt, when the mountains answered it in a prolonged roar which almost deafened us, for Rigi and Frohnalp and Uri Rothstock were lifting up their deep-toned voices in a hoarse appeal to God.

The waves ran so high now, and our frail boat was rocked so violently in the awful cradle of the deep, that we could hardly keep our seats at all, and the oars fell from my hands. Moppert was praying alone as we knelt down together with clasped hands. I could not pray. My mind was full of strange thoughts—yet not strange, perhaps, there, upon the threshold of eternity.

For I thought how short my life had been, and how sinfully wasted, and of how little value was my million of inheritance at this supreme moment—an inheritance which would not buy even one short day wherein to repent.

Thought how little worth was anything that men deem valuable—worldly honour,

worldly riches, name and fame. Thought of
that treasure in heaven, which my nurse had
told me was the only thing of any importance
for human beings who must die.

Thought of that dear nurse herself, with her
soft rippling hair, and gentle face, and strong
hands, forcing me to be good. Thought of her
one burst of passion, and her penitence, and of
the cruel thing that weaned a brother from a
sister, and must answer that.

Thought of my long-forgotten nursery high
up among the chimney-pots, with its one print
of sick Lazarus at the rich man's gate.
Thought of a girl's saucy face and sobbing
longing to be good, and of a French *chanson*
and its gay refrain.

Thought of my neglected sisters, and of
my father in Ballyacora Hall, and of what
they would say when the news of my death
reached them. And of the duke's daughter,
to whom I should never be married after all.

Thought of my noble friends and of the life to which they had introduced me, and of a certain *billet doux* in my dressing-case with a burning cheek yet. Thought of certain floggings at Eton, and of the pattern of the paper in my room at home, and of the dinner I had ordered at the hotel and which would never be eaten, and of Aileen's moist kisses on my cheek.

Thought of Patsey my groom, and of the licking I had given him, and whether he would remember or whether he would forget. Thought of a thousand things as ridiculous as these, until I laughed aloud, with my hand still in Moppert's and our boat still rocking in that awful cradle of the deep.

Thought of the beautiful lady on the promenade at Lucerne, and of the devil beside her, until, looking up, I saw them both—I swear it—the tears yet undried upon her cheeks, his lips white with passion, hers with terror.

Then I cried out to Moppert, for this last was more than I could endure.

As I cried, something struck us a terrible blow. Our boat rose right up in the water, and then fell back again, casting us into the seething abyss. I lost my hold of Moppert in a fierce struggle to retain something I was losing—I hardly knew what. Then the struggle ceased, and I fell into a deep sleep. And oh, what perfect rest, what peace wondrous and inexpressible came to me with death!

CHAPTER XIII.

A NEW THÉRÈSE.

Ach ! so grenzt des Geistes höh'res Leben
Oft an Tod, und ohne Wiederkehr
Sinkt, wenn wir am bessern Daseyn schweben,
Psyche tief hinab ins Sinnenmeer !
Selig, wem des Herzens Flammentriebe
Früh sich läutern zu der reineren Liebe !

K. W. JUSTI.

WHAT a dream I had had, to be sure ! Not
of *her* either ; all about the nearly forgotten
Thérèse and that foolish French *chanson* of
hers. The refrain was in my ears when I
awoke ; soft and low, as if being still sung in
the years that were gone.

'Tra la la !' Where was I, pray? Where
had I been last?

Memory, although shaky and confused, appeared in answer to the summons. Where had I been last? Why, at the bottom of Lucerne, dead as a stone!

True; then where was I now? In heaven or in—the other place?

I listened. There were sounds falling on my ear besides the distant sound of song— harsh, unmelodious, guttural sounds. Bass and shrill treble. A man's voice and a woman's.

Do people remain men and women in heaven? No, we have Biblical authority for asserting that they neither marry nor are given in marriage there, but are as the angels. This, then, was—the other place.

Oh, how their hard hands hurt me! how mercilessly they pulled me hither and thither! how they mouthed and maltreated the noble language of the fatherland!

And now the distant song swelled, coming

nearer and nearer, until at last it resolved
itself into words :

> A la fêt' du hameau,
> Ah ! comm' c'est beau !
> Tout's les filles
> Vont, au son du violon,
> Su' l'vert gazon
> Danser en rond :
> Tra, dera, la, la, la, la, la, la, la,
> N'faut pas danser comme ça,
> la, la ;
> L'Amour vous attend là.

. . . .

Then this was purgatory.

No, it was heaven after all ! A new presence was bending over me. A new atmosphere, delicately perfumed—ugh ! the former
had been smoke-sullied—saluted my nose. A
glow was rising to my face in glad response to
a warm ray of sunshine.

I raised my heavy lids and dimly saw a
rainbow face : two smiling eyes in which tears
yet sparkled, the whitest of pearly teeth
gleaming between coral lips.

'Thérèse,' I said, 'is this heaven, and are you dead too?'

I say, I *said*, but it was only my lips which moved, no sound was audible.

'See, Väterli; see, Fleurette; he is moving, he is trying to speak! He will not die!' cried an eager voice. Then arose a hubbub of sound, during which my mind wandered off again into a region where thought is not. A horror of great darkness fell upon me, in the midst of which I was only sensible of a struggle back to the light.

It was a man's voice which penetrated the shadows afresh and opened anew a window in my brain. He spoke the Swiss *patois*, but slowly and carefully, as if his tongue had not always been accustomed to the gutturals.

'The Herr Doctor was not at home, sayest thou?'

'No, father, but I left word that he should come.'

'Thou went away crying and came back singing, *Mädel*. Thou art like thy dead mother, who died because she couldn't sing any more.'

'Ah, that would kill me too,' said the girl.

'I believe thee well. But see, the gentleman is opening his eyes again—a foolish Englishman whom Providence has cared for beyond his deserts, doubtless.'

'He—he does not look foolish,' said the girl, charming open my heavy lids anew, as she bent over me and gently touched my face with her hand.

'You are better. You are safe,' she cried with confidence. 'We hardly want the doctor now.'

To which I answered slowly and painfully:

'Thérèse, why did you go away, and why have you come back to me?'

And I added, striving hard to be heard:

'And why do you speak this ugly language, instead of your own which is so soft and musical?'

'*Er kennt mich ja!*' she cried, amazed. 'Yes, I am Thérèse; how do you know it?'

'He is wandering in his mind,' said the man, advancing nearer to me. Then he continued in loud, emphatic English:

'I am an Englishman, sir. Me and some others pulled you out of the lake an hour or two ago. 'Twas a close shave, but it's all right now.'

Not all right. Anything but right. For as surely as the other was Thérèse, so surely this was William. I tried to rise, but was so tightly bound that I could not.

'Am I alive?'

'Ay, alive sure enough, and if not kicking yet, you will be soon, doubtless.'

Kicking! Had I any legs to kick with? I was conscious of none.

'Give him a drop of cherry brandy,' said the man, turning to speak to someone behind him; 'he's going again. And, Thérèse, run and open the door, *Mädel*. I hear the doctor coming at last.'

These were the last intelligible words I heard during many and many a day.

For Feeling, angry at her long banishment, now came back with a rush, running fiercely through every tortured nerve, and leaving behind her a burning track of pain.

The other senses fled while she racked me, or remained behind only to confound and mislead.

At last Feeling, tired of her cruel work, paused to rest, and I fell into a deep sleep.

It was evening when I awoke, roused from slumber by a distant murmur of many voices, the flowing of water, and certain dull thuds which were incomprehensible. I listened until

curiosity overcame listlessness, and I opened
my eyes to try if I could see.

A dimly burning lamp, depending from a
beam in the ceiling, gave light enough to show
that I was lying on a narrow bed in a large,
barely furnished room, and so closely smothered
in blankets and loaded with coverlets that it
was no wonder I could not move. An empty
chair stood by my bedside, a huge wardrobe
and huger stove completed the furniture. On
the wooden, roughly carved walls hung some
prints of impossible Virgins and impossible
Infants. At the foot of my bed stood a
woman, short and dumpy, low-browed and
long-chinned, contemplating me with the dull
stare of soulless curiosity. As my eyes met
those of this woman she opened her mouth
wider than they, but uttered not a word.

Between wardrobe and stove was a door
slightly ajar, through which issued the sounds
I have mentioned and also the fumes of un-

mistakable tobacco smoke and the smell of *Lagerbier*. As I looked and pondered, this door opened further still, admitting the tall, slight figure of a maiden.

'Fleurette,' she said softly, 'one has need of thee.'

This maiden was dressed in a short blue petticoat and scarlet *Mieder* (bodice), the latter tightly laced over as exquisite a bust as sculptor ever modelled. Her shoulders and dimpled arms were bare. Her shapely little feet hardly seemed to touch the ground they trod on, while her rich black hair, tied with a scarlet ribbon, fell in one broad plait far below her waist.

Thérèse! Thérèse in Swiss costume! I was certain of it. The same mobile face; the same saucy poise of the head; the same contradictory and ever-changing expression, for at first the brown eyes were laughing, while the lips remained sedate and grave; and now

the eyes swam in tears and the lips were
smiling.

Thérèse. Why had she come back to me,
now that another love had taken possession of
my heart?

William too. William, looking over her
shoulder with a grave, benevolent satisfaction,
right into my face. I should hardly have
shared this satisfaction but for the other love
I spoke of. Now I did, and smiled my con-
gratulations.

'How I hated you once, William,' I said,
as a second masculine head—a young and
handsome one—appeared in the doorway, and
an impatient masculine voice summoned back
Thérèse. The beer, the voice said, was hardly
worth the drinking without the *Mädel*.

'But now,' I added, magnanimously, 'I
congratulate you with all my heart.' And I
tried to lift the heavy bedclothes and to put
out my hand.

'Sir,' he said, amazed, 'I am William, doubtless, but I do not know you from Adam.'

'I used to pinch your calves,' I said, looking down at those members, now shrunk and lean.

He looked down at them himself and then at me, and his amazement deepened.

'I'm all abroad yet,' he said ; 'I can't make neither head nor tail of it.'

'Do you remember going away in a cab with Thérèse, and a little passionate boy looking on, full of rage and grief?'

'Ah-h !'

'And a gloomy London house with fog outside often, and always fog within ?'

'Ah-h-h !'

'I am glad you married her, William. I am glad you seem so happy and comfortable. I am glad——'

But my magnanimity was checked by a sudden reflection. I looked again at William.

Some seventeen years had passed since I last saw him, and their footsteps were plainly enough traced upon his bronzed face; whereas Thérèse was younger, brighter, prettier than ever.

'She is not your wife, is she?' I inquired, somewhat confusedly.

'My wife died sixteen year ago—sixteen year ago,' he repeated, with a deep sigh.

'And *this* Thérèse?'

'This Thérèse'—and now his hard face softened, and a radiant light came into his eyes—'this one is my little *Mädel*—my *Töchterlein*.'

It was my turn now to utter a long-drawn 'Ah!'

'I reckon I know you now,' he continued, 'and I thank God A'mighty once more that 't was me as drew you out of the water, for *she* were fond of you.'

He paused again, putting his hand to his

furrowed brow as if the word had aroused a host of painful recollections; then continued in a more cheerful voice :

' You *was* a Tartar in them days, Master Charles, sure enough. Such a little chap too to be so much in love! I've laughed about it many a time with her, until we both laughed no longer, because——'

He broke off anew to put one arm around his daughter's waist and lift the other to her round cheek as she came up to his side. How oddly the action affected me as they stood thus a moment together—the new William and the old Thérèse !

CHAPTER XIV.

MY LITTLE MISTRESS.

Cari sunt liberi, propinqui, familiares: sed omnes omnium caritates patria una complexa est.—CICERO, *De Officiis.*

WE became very good friends in due time, this Thérèse and I. For it was she who nursed me, aided by William, until I could stand upon my own shaky legs again.

I wonder if there is any connection for the time, except that of husband and wife, more close and intimate than the connection of patient and nurse? I wonder if there is any more dangerous, when both are young?

Not that there was any danger for us—

not the remotest. I had made her my confidante. I had enlisted her warm sympathies on behalf of the beautiful, unfortunate lady whom I loved.

Whom I loved. Is love necessarily the growth of months? Can it not spring up, like Jonah's gourd, in a night?

It did not in the least interfere with my liking for my pretty nurse. I liked well, I confess it, to see her by my bedside. I liked her tyranny. I liked our daily quarrels, specially when they were over. Above all, I liked—couldn't have done without—the makings-up.

I had found out the meaning of the mysterious thuds, and why tobacco smoke and *Lagerbier* perpetually perfumed the place. William was owner and landlord of a small public-house (*Schenke*), a favourite resort for men of all ages. Thérèse was its pretty, feminine attraction.

It was morning. The sunshine was streaming in warm and bright through the diamond - shaped window-panes, tinging Thérèse's black hair with a golden glitter and making the knitting-needles in her busy hand twinkle like fireflies as they flashed hither and thither in the light.

A question which had haunted me for long—ever since I could think at all of other than my pain—hovered on my lips, but, like a coward, lacked courage to go further.

'Thérèse,' I said, breaking the silence in order to brace myself, ' to-day I really feel as if I were going to get better.'

' *Ei, natürlich,*' she answered, laughing, ' we never meant to let you die, monsieur.'

I watched the grey stocking lengthening in her hands, resolving to speak at every turn. Thrice I even uttered an inarticulate sound ; thrice Thérèse's bright eyes were turned towards me, and her rosy lips opened to an

'*Eh, monsieur?*' thrice I cleared my throat, and made believe that that was all I wanted.

'If you will be good, monsieur,' said Thérèse, after consulting my watch and forcing me to swallow two tablespoonfuls of a disgusting mixture — enjoying my sufferings, the minx, with all her heart—and won't get excited, why perhaps I'll tell you something.'

Perhaps, forsooth! That was her way of tormenting me. Nevertheless, a touch of earnestness in her saucy voice made me turn pale and tremble.

'*Ei! ei!* if you are going to look like that, monsieur, I'll run away and send old Fleurette to come and sit beside you. You will go off to sleep again like a lamb with Fleurette; for'—with an irresistible little grimace—'it makes one sleepy only to look at her.'

'Wait till I am well, *mein Fräulein*, and

see if I don't pay you out then for your treatment of me now.'

'Treatment! *Der Herr hat gut sprechen.* I should like to know who would have given him his drops so regularly, or mixed his mustard plasters so strong, or applied the leeches to his aching temples, if *I* hadn't been there!'

'*Grausames Geschöpf!* It is to you, then, that I am indebted for the tortures inflicted upon me! Never mind, I promise not to forget it.'

'No fear of that,' said Thérèse, tossing her pretty head and threatening me with a sharp-pointed knitting-needle. '*Die Herren Engländer* are known all the world over for their profound memory for injuries, and the extreme shortness of their memories for benefits they have received. Even my father, who has lived long enough with warmer-hearted folk to know better, never remembers my good deeds when he is angry; but only the one little act, hardly worth noticing, which has aroused his ire.'

'It's easy to say that, but you forget, mam'selle, that you are half English yourself.'

'No, monsieur, not a quarter English, thank heaven! All my heart belongs to Switzerland, and if I had to live anywhere else I should pine away and die. My father tried, when I was little, to instil English dulness into me ; and tries, now that I am big, to scold me into being as hard and stiff and *kaltblütig* as his countrywomen. I have seen many of them in Lucerne, and you would think (for they are as cold and hard-looking as the *Gletscher* upon our mountains) that they had never learned to laugh or cry or sing or dance.'

She was at a stumbling-block in her stocking just now, and bent her dark head over it for a moment without speaking.

'*Ach!* only a slipped stitch, monsieur,

which reminds me that I have been told not to talk to you, and not to let you talk too much either.'

' *Unsinn*, maiden ! Go on.'

' Monsieur thinks he has but to command, and that of course Théreschen must obey. But Thérèse doesn't like to obey ; she likes to have someone to tease and torment all the livelong day. Ah, monsieur need not make such big eyes. I am as hard-hearted as a stone.'

' Wait till I am well again.'

' Besides,' she went on, ' what pleasure can it be to a warm-blooded Swiss girl to talk to a cold-blooded *Engländer*, or to try and make *him* understand what love of country means, nor with what joy and pride we Swiss look up to our noble mountains, knowing that there is nothing else half so beautiful on earth ? '

' What an impassioned little patriot it is ! '

'How you Englishmen must hate your England, monsieur, to run away from it as you do, as if there was pestilence in the very wind which blows over it. *Hu!* I have heard of it—a dark, grey country, where there is neither summer nor winter; only fog and mist and smoke. France is better than that, though not half so good as Switzerland. Wouldn't monsieur give half of his fortune, now, to have been born in this wonderful country of ours?'

'England is a more wonderful country still, Thérèse.'

'Oh, I will not talk to monsieur any more. I will sing a French *chanson*, as gay as the song of a skylark; all about love and laughter, where the woods dance to the measure. Monsieur would make me else, in the twinkling of an eye, as dull and dismal as he is himself. I had nearly lost my temper. I will go look for it, and find it again in a song.'

How wonderfully pretty the girl looked,
as she broke out in a gleeful melody, her
dark eyes flashing, her cheeks bright with
unwonted colour (she had inherited her
mother's southern clear sallowness), and the
sunshine playing hide-and-seek in her raven
hair! Now in words, now in song, how
continuously and uninterruptedly the sparkling stream flowed from between her scarlet
lips! I forgot everything again but lazy
pleasure and content as I lay watching
her.

'It is strange,' she continued, after a short
pause—while I observed, and wondered at it,
that when she was silent her hands ceased
to work too, and when the stream of talk
bubbled out most irrepressibly her fingers
played a quick accompaniment—'it is strange,
though, that my father will talk of "Old
England"'—these last two words were brought
out with the prettiest foreign accent imagin-

able—' as if he loved it, and my grandmother wore out her old heart in pining for
la belle France!   Monsieur, why do you
sigh?   You are disobeying me and getting
excited.'

'You have not told me yet what you said
you would.'

'Because you are not good.   Your cheek
is flushed ; perhaps a leech——'

'I am not going to stand it.   If you
venture to bring one of the horrible creatures
into the room——'

'Monsieur, there is a bottle of them in
the cupboard.'

'Then I desire that they are instantly
thrown into the lake.'

'Thrown into the lake!   Why it would
be as much as my life is worth to attempt it.
I know I should be thrown in after them.
But, perhaps, that, too, is what Monsieur
desires.'

'I desire that you will sit down beside me again and tell me instantly the news you promised.'

'*O Weh! O Weh!* I never thought to find the tales I have heard of English ingratitude so speedily verified. Yesterday, and all the days before, it was: "*Liebe Thérèse, bitte, bitte,*" or "*Théreschen, du bist mein rettender Engel,*" or "*Kind, ich werde nie vergessen was du mir gethan,*" and to-day, nothing but desires and commands and threats. Oh, *die Herren Engländer* are all the same, every one of them! I will go and cook the *Suppe* and send Fleurette, who is as deaf as a post, to come and sit beside you.'

'Send Fleurette at your peril,' I rejoined, seizing the perverse little hand and pressing it to my lips. 'And now that I have you fast, tell me the news this moment.'

What a strange girl she was! her mood as variable as the zigzag flight of the swallow.

She had been scolding me before with a contradictory sparkle in her eye; now it flashed out a lightning ray, and her lip quivered. She rose up from her seat by my bedside as haughtily as an offended princess.

'What is the matter, Thérèse?'

'Monsieur is not in England,' she answered, turning away her flushing cheek, 'and will have to learn that his commands are not law in Switzerland. Sit down again? Certainly not, until monsieur has learned to control himself a little, and to behave like a gentleman.'

'Good heavens! what have I done?'

'Done! Is monsieur lord of Europe that he ventures to assume a tone so arrogant—to command where he should obey?'

'Well,' I said, falling back upon my pillow, 'the man who marries you will have his hands full?'

'And the woman who marries you,

monsieur, had need be born without a heart.
at all.'

'I've nothing further to say, Thérèse.'

'Nor have I. Except—except that I was
told not to excite you; and your cheek is
flushed, and your eye bright, and your breathing hurried and unequal. Let me give you
your medicine, monsieur, and let us quarrel
when you are better.'

She was looking at me now with a softened
and a troubled eye, and the hand with which
she smoothed my pillow trembled a little. I
was quick to seize my advantage, and cunning
enough to try a new form of inducement.

'Thérèschen, you can make some allow-
ance for a sick man, cannot you? I am
afraid of the news you have promised me, but
I am still more afraid of the uncertainty. It
is that which is agitating me. Be good to me,
Thérèse. *Do* tell me.'

'There,' she said, smiling, yet pricked to

the quick by my tone of supplication, 'you have given me tit for tat with a vengeance, monsieur. I am as submissive to your *do* as I was impervious to your *must*. But get agitated at your peril! The moment you begin, I am gone.'

How could I help getting agitated? My heart began to beat quick and fast; my eyes grew dim. Yet surely she had no bad news to communicate. Surely no one could contemplate the terrible solemnity of death with those laughing eyes and that dimpling cheek.

'You will let me take up the heel of my stocking first, will you not, monsieur?' she said, 'and then I can talk on without interruption.'

But this was a little too strong a strain on my endurance. I broke down under it, and cried out petulantly: 'If you only knew, Thérèse, what I have suffered, how terribly I have been racked by alternate hope and fear, you would not have the heart——'

Here my new weapon fell so heavily on her that she winced and paled under it, for my voice was choked with a sob, and the tears were rising.

She had thrown down her knitting instantly, and now knelt by my bedside in the completeness of her penitence ; her bare dimpled elbows on the counterpane, her sweet remorseful face supported by a pair of shapely hands—hands more accustomed to cuff than to caress, but oh! so thrilling in their contact when they did!—her dark eyes meeting mine full of a sweet motherly relenting, as if they would plead, ' My teasing was all love upside-down,' while her voice, when she spoke, was as soft as that of any cooing dove.

' You will break my heart if you look at me like that, monsieur ; you must know that I would not really hurt you for the world. Have I been so very cruel to you ? If it had been

news of the fair lady, I wouldn't have kept it
from you for an instant, for I can guess how
eager you would have been for them—but a
little old man, *kaum grösser als ich*, how could
I imagine that your heart was so set on him?
—one of a nation, too, who are the sworn
enemies of your England.'

I could not speak. So *he* had been saved
too, by a miracle!

'*Ruhig! ruhig!* monsieur. You have no
need to be afraid. Did you think so badly of
Thérèse as to believe she could tease you
about so solemn and sad a thing as that you
feared? He is to come again this afternoon to
see you, if the doctor finds you are none the
worse for the intelligence. That was why
I took so many precautions in telling you.
And I would ask you to forgive me, only that
I am still a little angry that you could think
so badly of me.'

She looked at me smiling, but I could not

smile yet. I was vehemently struggling with tears, and getting worsted by them. Remember, in my excuse, how weak I was.

'He has seen you once before, monsieur,' continued Thérèse, still upon her knees. 'I led him to the door between this and the *Schenkstube*, and let him look in upon you as you slept, and he cried—the little man—*lieber Gott!* as you are crying now.'

Then she broke down herself, and we cried together as heartily and noisily as two children. And (how it happened I do not know) my hot head was on her bosom, and our lips so close, *so close*, that at last they touched involuntarily, separating again with a sound which startled us into quietude.

The next moment she was gone, and I alone, to wonder what we had done, and what was the meaning of it, and why forbidden fruit is always the sweetest.

But when she came, half an hour after-

wards, to administer the *Suppe* cooked by
Fleurette, there was no sign of shame on her
pale oval cheek, or of embarrassment in her
laughing eye. She was the old Thérèse
again ; in a dozen moods at once ; per-
emptory, supplicating ; haughty, humble ;
sweet as honey and bitter as quinine ;
sharp and gentle in a breath ; irresistible, in
short, to any man whose heart was not pre-
occupied as mine was.

But the kiss was forgotten, or ignored
completely. Mademoiselle was full of her
function, and harnessed with its authority to
the unflinching finger-tips. She approached
my bed with a resolute air, and stationed
herself beside it with the rigidity and deter-
mination of a sentinel on duty.

'Open your mouth, monsieur.' The tone
of her voice was pregnant with an authority
which seemed to challenge opposition.

I accepted the challenge instantly, and

threw down a ready gauntlet. Next to kiss-
ing Thérèse, nothing was pleasanter than
quarrelling with her. At least at the moment I thought so.

'What for, *mein Fräulein*?'

'Asks "What for?" when I am standing
with the spoon in one hand and the steaming
basin in the other! But men are as blind as
moles, especially Englishmen.'

'And chits, pretending to be women, are
as perverse as young fillies till they are
tamed by bit and bridle — especially cos-
mopolites, half Swiss, half English, and half
French.'

'Three halves in a whole—is that an
English problem, monsieur? Even our village
Lehrer taught me better than that. And,
talking of bits and bridles, there *is* such a
thing as a good Swiss *Ruthe*.'

'Certainly, *mein Fräulein*. I hardly liked

to suggest it; but if you are sensible that your iniquities rise to that alternative——'

'You asked me "What for?" just now, monsieur, but I will tell you what *not* for. Not to talk certainly, and not to——' Here she stopped, blushing: a singularly infectious blush, for my cheek instantly reflected it, and our eyes fell simultaneously. Thérèse was the first to recover her lost self-possession. In some things women are a thousand times cleverer than men.

'Do you think the newly hatched nestlings ask "What for?" when the parent birds bring the worm?' said Thérèse in atone of sharp reprimand. 'Open your mouth this moment, or——'

In defiance of the threatening '*sonst*,' I only opened it to speak again:

'But I am not hungry, and am not a newly hatched nestling, and if anybody offered me a worm——'

'No credit to you,' interrupted Thérèse, suddenly putting down her basin, and shifting her spoon in a manner which made me remember with some alarm my old nurse, and the way in which she would sometimes, after long waiting, administer medicine ; ' you might have been, you know.'

This logic being unanswerable, as woman's logic always is, I was dumb. Moreover, the power of speech was momentarily taken from me : my nurse's manner of coercion was not, I found, peculiar to any nation, but the common property of all ; the spoon was in my mouth, and it was a case of swallowing or choking. So I submitted in somewhat shamefaced silence, and the *Suppe* being remarkably good, and my appetite only emotionally in abeyance and now coming fresh to the fore, I resented the finale almost as much as I had resented the brusque commencement.

' Is that all?' I inquired, as the spoon ceased

to travel from the basin to my mouth, and
Thérèse's busy hands were arranging the
pillows at my head.

'That is all, monsieur.'

'But I have not had half enough.'

'Can't help it, monsieur; you will not get
any more.'

'One might think I was a baby.'

'One might really often think so,' said
Thérèse, with ready acquiescence.

I was too sleepy to be angry. So I looked
up into the bright face of my *Mütterchen*, and
she looked down on me, firm, though smiling.

'Little tyrant!' I murmured.

'Tyrant indeed!' And I saw the pretty
head toss just as my eyes were closing. 'But
what could you expect from an *Engländer*?
And now, monsieur, you are to go to sleep
this minute.'

I am not sure whether I only thought
or spoke the next words, to the effect that

nothing should induce me. I only know that I did go to sleep, perhaps because I knew that Thérèse was not to be disobeyed with impunity; and slept as sweetly and peacefully as if I had been in truth the baby Thérèse loved to make of me. And I dreamed I was a doll, and that the *Mädel* was my little mistress; that sometimes she beat and sometimes caressed me,—always holding me though, so that chastisement and reward were as like as two peas, and hardly distinguishable,—very close to her heart.

CHAPTER XV.

THÉRÈSE.

Wouldst be loved by all the world,
  Maiden, sweet as May in bloom,
Leave thy rosy lip uncurled,
  Rest contented with thy doom.

Know that, Envy hateth most
  What is lovely, sweet and fair ;
Know it is thy virtues' host
  That she cannot, cannot bear.

I SLEPT well after hearing the good news from Thérèse, and when the morning sun streamed in again through the diamond-shaped panes, Moppert was allowed to come into my room. My eyes were too dim to see him for a moment, but when they cleared, we clasped hands and gazed into one another's faces as friends might do, meeting in Eternity.

Then he sat down beside me, with a warning finger on his lip, and a look of such sincere affection in his eyes that my own filled again.

'Ah, dear friend,' he said, 'I have offered up a thousand prayers to Our Lady on your behalf, and that they have been answered seems to me a blessed omen for the future.'

I noticed with pain that he was replacing his right arm in a sling from which he had removed it during our hand-shake.

'Nothing of consequence' he explained, 'only a sprain which is all but healed again.'

'How did it happen?'

'*Mon ami*, I will tell you everything in time, but to-day I have been severely restricted as to the topic of our discourse, and it seems to me that mademoiselle is a little person who expects to be obeyed.

I laughed and nodded, very emphatically.

'Ah, monsieur, you have had a hard time

of it no doubt with this little brunette? She
has ruled you with a rod of iron?'

'Not with one, monsieur, but with ten.'

'Pommelled you sore, eh?'

'Monsieur, I am one wound from head to
foot.'

'*La coquine!* And has she inflicted more
than flesh-wounds, monsieur? Has she tried
her hand upon your heart?'

'Monsieur, I cannot tell what she might
have done; she is capable of *anything*, but I
have no heart left to wound.'

'Did you leave it behind you in the lake
for the water nixies?'

'You know better than that, monsieur;
you know where it is.'

'The cold water has not quenched your
ardour then? You still think of the other?'

'Oh, monsieur, if you only knew how
often and how much!'

'*Mon ami*, your cheek is flushing and

your eye brightening. It is good. I am
content to see˙ it. But you must not let
Mademoiselle Thérèse misunderstand you;
her giddy head might get some absurd idea
into it, which would grieve you, would it
not?'

He looked keenly at me as he put the
question. I answered impetuously:

'Monsieur, it would grieve me so much,
that if I feared anything of the sort, I would
ask you to help me don my coat and pantaloons, and lend me a helping hand to run
away.'

'There is no danger then?'

'I am very fond of Thérèse, monsieur, and
I think she likes me too a little, though she
is so hard with me.'

'Humph!'

I˙ went on recklessly, an irresistible im-
pulse driving me to confess.

'We quarrel, but we make it up again,

and yesterday we solemnised our reconcilia-
tion with a kiss.'

'What! You have dared to embrace
her!'

'Yes, monsieur. We are capital friends,
Thérèse and I. I like her as well as if she
were my sister. And she has a pretty mouth ;
don't you think so ? '

'Man without a conscience ; here is your
coat, here are your pantaloons ; put them on
this minute.'

'Monsieur, I would rather be excused.
On the whole, I feel too weak to move yet.
This bed is not of down, yet my limbs have
ceased to ache, and now it seems easy. And
if my pretty nurse teases me, why, I can pay
her out in kisses.'

'And be paid out by her father in coin
less sweet but much more wholesome. Well,
I *had* hopes of you.'

'Cherish them still, monsieur, for I have

great hopes of myself. I have left my *ennui* behind me in the lake. There is work for me to do. The first work, with God's help, to save her.'

'Which her?' inquired Moppert, a doubtful sparkle in his eye.

'Was there never a time, monsieur, when for you, as for me, the feminine pronoun meant only one person—meant all the world, in short?'

'Ah, the poor Thérèse!'

'Do you think I would have kissed her, or she me, if we had not both known——'

'If you had both known that a horse-whipping was in store for you, it would have been a wholesome reminder; and, as for me, I would not lift a finger to prevent it.'

'Yes, you would, monsieur, for my pulse never throbbed a throb quicker when our lips met.'

'But hers, hers, hers?'

'Here she comes to answer for herself.'

The door was opening as I spoke, and Thérèse's laughing eyes met mine inquiringly.

'Thérèse, come and take my part. This friend of mine has been doing nothing but scold me.'

'Been scolding you, has he? Well, I have no doubt you deserve it. But if scolding won't do, we must try punishment. He has been getting excited, is it not so, monsieur? Therefore you will have the kindness to wish him good-bye.'

'Excited? My blood is flowing as icily as your own, mademoiselle. When you hear what he has been saying, you will want to punish him instead of me.'

Moppert made a horrified gesture at my temerity. But I thought I knew what I was doing.

'What do you think he's afraid of?' I said, laughing.

'Of your taking cold and of my being angry,' she answered, peremptorily replacing my head upon the pillow from which I had raised it. 'Who gave you leave to sit up, monsieur?'

'Leave? Can't I please myself?'

'Certainly not,' answered Thérèse, laying one cool hand upon my brow, and feeling my pulse with the other.

It was delightful. I hardly like to say how delightful, it seems so inconsistent.

'Am I not my own master?' I continued, pretending to rebel in order to prolong the punishment.

She did not deign to answer, only ran her slender fingers through my hair, and stooped low to listen to my breathing. Her pretty mouth, temptingly rounded, almost touched mine.

Yet I felt sure, quite, quite sure, that her love for me was entirely motherly.

' Perhaps he was afraid of that,' repeated Thérèse, ' and with excellent reason too, for you *are* feverish and I *am* angry.'

' No, mademoiselle, it wasn't that at all,' I went on, laughing ; ' he was afraid of your falling in love with me ; but now that he sees how you behave to me, I think his fears will vanish.'

For a moment after I had made this foolish, foolish speech, there was a dead silence. Angry colour flushed Thérèse's cheek a deep crimson, her restless hands half clenched themselves, and her dark eyes flashed. Then she turned and walked to the door between us and the *Schenkstube*, standing there a moment before turning back to us.

The colour had faded from her cheek again, leaving it paler than usual, and her mouth, in the corners of which a smile always seemed to lurk, was sternly set—sternly and yet so

sorrowfully that I wished I had bitten off my
tongue before letting it wag so foolishly.

She seated herself on a chair by my bedside, first chastising me with a look which
made me tingle from head to foot with shame,
then turned her beautiful eyes, dark, clear, and
unwontedly earnest, on Moppert, to whom she
spoke. He had been looking at her with undisguised admiration, at me with undisguised
reproof.

'Monsieur,' she began, somewhat irrele-
vantly as I thought, 'you have been now nearly
a fortnight in Brunnen, and have, no doubt,
often heard people speak of Thérèse, the
Schenkmädchen?'

'Mademoiselle, I have heard you spoken
of more than anyone else in Brunnen.'

'Monsieur, your hair is grey—an old man
surely would not deceive a girl who trusted
in him—and your eyes are grave and clear

and steady. I believe in eyes. I believe that I may trust you.'

'Mademoiselle, if my eyes are a true index to my heart, you may trust them implicitly, for that would scorn to deceive you.'

'Tell me then, tell me truly, what you have heard about Thérèse.'

'Mademoiselle, I have heard much that is good. I have heard that you are very beautiful, and I see that it is true—the most beautiful girl in all the four cantons.'

Was she beautiful? I had hardly thought about it before. I only knew that she was pleasant. But now, looking at her with newly awakened eyes, I saw that it was true. Not only the most beautiful girl in the four cantons, but also, save one, the most beautiful woman in the world. Well for me that I had been in love before I saw her. For even to my chastened pride the thought of marrying a *Schenkmädchen* was preposterous.

Yet how gracefully, and now how haughtily, her small head sat upon her shapely neck! How smooth and dimpled were her shoulders! How white the full plumpness of her arms! How exquisitely curled the scarlet lips, scornful as those of any titled dame! Where, in the name of all the blue blood in the universe, did the ex-footman's daughter learn to look like that?

'Go on, monsieur. Do they say that I am sweet-tempered? Do they say——' Here she broke down with a smothered cry of angry and indignant pain.

'No, mademoiselle, but they say that your voice is sweeter than that of the far-famed Loreley, and that you lure men to destruction.'

'What more?'

'Let me stop, mademoiselle. It is not true, I am sure.'

'Monsieur, you have promised me.'

'That then you change your note and laugh at the hearts you have broken.'

'They say that, do they? Go on.'

'Mademoiselle, let me stop, I beseech you. Your bodice is rising and falling stormily; on your cheek one spot begins to glow like a coal of fire; your smooth forehead is contracting; your slipper restless.'

'Monsieur, I am not going to fly into a passion. I can control myself, and I will.'

'Mademoiselle, if you command me to proceed I have no choice but to obey. They say further—— Mademoiselle, let it be enough; what does it matter?'

'I *will* hear it.'

'Mademoiselle, you are cruel to me as well as to yourself. You do not know what you are asking.'

'But I *will* hear it.'

'They say that you are only nursing the Englishman to break his heart too; that there

is witchery in your charms, and that no man
can withstand you. They say that you have
no heart to love anyone, and that he had
better have been drowned in the lake than
ever come near you. They have sent me to
take him away.'

The long kept back tears were coming at
last. I saw them falling one by one. I saw
the girl's struggle to keep back the sobs
shaking her. And I had to remember that
this was all my doing.

'So you have come to take him away,'
she said at last, with as much bitterness as
she could infuse into the sweet tones of her
voice.

'I won't be taken away, Thérèse—not if he
brings everyone in Brunnen to help him.'

She smiled at me through her tears, even
in the midst of her agitation carefully putting back the hand I stretched out under
the coverlet again.

'Oh, monsieur, monsieur,' she cried, laughing, now almost her old bright self once
more, 'you come too late. The mischief is
done already. He will not go, even though I
bid him.'

'I shall never get well without the tonic
of your tyranny,' I cried.

'You hear, monsieur. Is it not dreadful?
Don't you wish he had been left at the
bottom of the lake?'

'No, mademoiselle.'

'Don't you wish he had never seen
Thérèse?'

'No, mademoiselle; I esteem him fortunate, and myself too, for having had that
pleasure.'

'Ah, perhaps you are falling a victim
yourself!'

'Yes, mademoiselle, I have been falling a
victim ever since I saw you.'

'You frighten me, monsieur. I did not

know I was so dangerous, nor that I could break hearts so easily.'

'Mademoiselle, necks have been broken in scaling your mountains, but that is not the fault of the glacier.'

'Bah! Would you compare me to anything so icy as that? You think then, like my kind neighbours, that I have no heart at all.'

'I think, mademoiselle, that a heart capable of profoundest affection beats beneath your *Mieder*—a heart that loving once would love for ever, but that as yet it is untouched.'

As she put her hands upon his shoulders in the pretty way in which she was wont to plead with her father, I saw her face change its expression from that of a playful child to that of an impassioned woman. Her pale cheek glowed again, her lips parted, her voice was agitated, as if an unskilful hand had touched some exquisite instrument which could not yet yield full harmony.

'Will it ever be touched?' she said, her voice vibrating, while she looked up into the old man's face as if he had been a prophet; 'will it ever be touched, monsieur?'

But before he could answer she was laughing again gaily, promising me no end of penalties for having been the cause of so much disquietude, and laughed still as she playfully pushed Moppert out of my room into the glowing sunshine of the mid-day.

CHAPTER XVI.

A SOLEMN VOW.

'O mon père,' lui dis-je, 'je ne savais pas que la direction d'intention eût la force de rendre les promesses utiles.' 'Vous voyez,' dit le père, 'que voilà une grande facilité pour le commerce du monde.'—PASCAL (*Lettres Provinciales*).

MY progress towards complete recovery was very rapid after my interview with Moppert. Soon I was allowed to sit up ; soon even able to take a few steps out into the sweet autumn air ; very soon able to coerce Thérèse, as I triumphantly asserted, instead of her coercing me.

But before this happy termination to our disaster had been attained, nearly a month had elapsed, during which our worst fears for the beautiful lady might have been realised.

And though I could not deny even to myself that her image in my mind had become somewhat misty, I struggled against the conviction with fierce contempt for my instability. Was it not to her that I owed the rousing of soul and body out of a lethargy which was ruining me? I hated myself for my enforced inaction, and every minute of delay seemed an age.

In the meantime Moppert had not been idle. He had been to Lucerne before he saw me, and ascertained that the apartments occupied by Monsieur le Prince de Pöbeldowski and his suite had been taken until the end of October, and that therefore we still had some time before us.

His inquiries concerning the lady herself had not produced any definite information. The bribed waiter, probably already bribed by some one else, was quite non-committal. He did not know where Mademoiselle came from; she spoke several languages equally well. He did not know whether the Princess was kind to her—the Prince was, and the Prince was master. He did not know whether she had any friends or not—never heard of any. He did not know whether she were happy—she cried a good bit, which was a queer way of showing it ; but then women were queer—could narrate a case in point from his own experience.

Furthermore the waiter, pulled up rather short at this point ; did not know—very sulkily—anything more about her—had too much to do to busy himself with what others were doing. Besides, as a respectable young man engaged to a respectable young woman, she wasn't the sort of person he cared to talk about.

And this was all Moppert's five francs had elicited.

'I wish I had been there to knock him down,' I cried indignantly.

'But as you were not,' said Moppert rather drily, ' what is to be done next?'

My own feelings would have prompted me to say, Raise the devil generally, but Moppert was still looking at me with his own dry caustic smile, and I was silent.

'I'll tell you what, *mon ami*,' he said, after a thoughtful tug at his moustache, ' when I was quite nonplussed at Lucerne I used to go to Madame Papillote, and she always knew what to do. Women beat us out and out at intrigue. Let us take a woman into our confidence.'

' What woman?'

' Who better than Mademoiselle Thérèse?'

I blushed a little. Was he thinking to kill two birds with one stone? But he was right; if anyone could help us it was she.

Thérèse listened as Moppert narrated, with grave attention, her eyes downcast, even her busy fingers perfectly motionless. I think he was somewhat reassured by her apathy, by her evident want of surprise.

'You did well,' she said at last, slowly, yet very composedly, 'you did well, monsieur, to come to Thérèse. People say that what I undertake I succeed in, and I am going to undertake to help you.'

'Thérèse,' I cried, enraptured, 'was there ever such a charming girl as you are? How shall I thank you?'

I stretched out my hand to grasp hers, but she did not seem to see it. I tried to catch her eye, but she appeared to have only vision for Moppert.

'Thérèse, tell me what you want most in the world; and I will give it you, even if it cost me half what I possess.'

With one of those sudden changes so characteristic of her, she now turned sharply towards me; her face, nay, even her white shoulders and pearly ears, dyed a deep crimson.

Her girlish figure shook with the violent effort she made to regain her lost self-control.   It seemed as if the effort would choke her.

'What is the matter, Thérèse?   What have I done to vex you?'

She burst into a peal of laughter—laughter so discordant that it horrified me—and ran, still laughing, out of the room.

I looked at Moppert for an explanation; but he only said sharply and laconically, as the door closed upon us :

'How soon will you be able to go?'

Adding, after a short interval, during which he fiercely tugged at his moustache :

'If ever you kiss that girl again I'll give up the enterprise.'

Could he have imagined——?

And I made a vow—a solemn one—never to kiss Thérèse again on any provocation what-soever, and kept it—of course.

CHAPTER XVII.

IN THE SCHENKSTUBE.

'And now, good day; I wish you pleasant dreams,
  And greater faith in woman.'

'Greater faith! I have the greatest faith ;
  For I *believe* Victorian is her lover.'—LONGFELLOW.

IN a few moments after that last angry remark from Moppert, William entered the room, bringing with him a stout Brunnen lad, who greeted me with a grin from ear to ear, and a gruff 'Grüss Gott, Herre.'

'Grüss Gott,' I answered, regarding with interest this burly son of the soil. His figure was almost gigantic, and even his loose and ill-made clothes could not quite disguise limbs shaped like those of a young Hercules. His coarse linen shirt, bleached white as the snow upon his own mountains, hung loose over his chest, leaving his massive throat and hairy breast visible. His hands and feet were immense. He was a far finer specimen of the human animal than an average English peasant, and, so far as I have had an opportunity of judging, no exception, but a type of his class in German Switzerland.

But, ascending from the throat to the head, where that intangible something, Human Intelligence, is supposed to have its seat, one would have given, without hesitation, the palm to the average Anglo-Saxon. The pale goggle blue eyes of the giant, innocent and pacific looking, seemed but a degree removed from those of a peaceful grazing ox, whose knowledge of the world's laws goes no higher than that ploughing comes before grazing, labour before repose.

Yet once I saw those dull orbs, on a never-to-be-forgotten occasion, all ablaze in the light of a divine fire, lit by God.

Globularity was the prevailing impression

which this gigantic Teuton made upon me. His face was round, his flat nose round, his mildly astonished eyes round. And as for his temper, as I found out afterwards, there wasn't an angle in it.

According to the law of contrariety which governs human actions, some one had bestowed the rather ferocious name of Nicholas upon this peaceful giant. He was known to his compatriots as Peter's Nick — Peter being his paternal ancestor. And although so young, he had already a Nick of his own, who is doubtless now known by the cognomen of Old Nick's Nick.

'Well, sir, how do you find yourself this evening?' said William kindly. 'Me and Nick's been sent to carry you into the *Schenkstube*. There's goin' to be some fun to-night. And she · bade us look sharp about it, did the *Mädel*, and if *we* don't *she* will. What did the *Mädel* say, Nick?'

'To bring him whether he would or no,' answered Nick, nothing now but a stalwart figure, capped by a mouth.

'And we are going to do it, Nick?'

'*Jo, jo, Herre.*'

If Thérèse had told Nick to throw me into the lake, he would have done it, I am sure.

The next moment I was in the air, easy chair and all, raised there by the sinewy arms of Nicholas, and a moment later I was in the *Schenkstube.*

Moppert, laughing heartily, followed me and my bearer.

We were greeted by a simultaneous: *Grüss Gott!* from about twenty to thirty men, from the bald-headed patriarch of the village to the lad, barely emancipated from the discipline of the maternal *Ruthe.*

There were three windows in the room— lattice-windows, with diamond-shaped panes.

One of these was open, and through it I looked down upon the shimmering lake, now dyed deep crimson by the glory of the sunset.

Opposite me rose the mountains, and I thought, as I gazed, that heaven itself could not be more divinely beautiful. No addition could improve the scene, and an item wanting would have been—at least to me—as disturbing as a feature failing on a lovely human face.

Feeling a trifle embarrassed by the universal gaze—for I was an object of great interest to the ' lads '—I occupied myself for a while solely with the beauty of the landscape, brightened into special glory by the brilliancy of the setting sun, which was framing the tops of the mountains opposite with a deep border of living and transparent gold.

The two arms of the lake, one stretching

towards Lucerne, the other towards Flüelen
—the so-called Lake of Uri—lay as calm and
unruffled before me as if they had never
known what it was to be lashed by the Föhn.
The water was of a vivid green, dark under
the shadow of the mountains ; and the air so
clear that I could see the crevices on the
glacier of Uri Rothstock, and even the point
where ice melted into water. A few boats
were crossing from the other side, wherein
sat youths and maidens, the former wearing
sprigs of edelweiss in their round hats, the
latter gaily attired in the blue and scarlet
Mieder of the national costume.

As I gazed, the sun sank lower, embracing
the mountains with ever-increasing ardour as
the moment drew near when he must go.
I saw the snow-tops crimson under his kisses
until they glowed like peaks of living fire.

'Is it not glorious, monsieur?' said
Thérèse, in a low voice at my ear. 'Don't you

think God must have a special love for
Switzerland ? '

I looked round with a sigh. Even her
sweet voice broke the spell.

' Monsieur, though I have seen it so often,
I always feel it just as new and wonderful. I
could fancy I saw the gates of heaven opening, and that in another moment we should
look straight in on God.'

The light was slowly fading now, and
Thérèse stood quietly beside me until the
mountains had recovered their usual proud
purity—all the colder, it seemed, after their
late outbreak of passion—and in the darkening sky stars began to twinkle. Then she
closed the window; ordering me, with that
quick change of feeling so characteristic of
her, not to sit apart, sullen and morose, any
longer, but to pay a little attention to my
neighbours.

In obedience to my little dictatress, I

commenced conversation with a stout
'*Junge*' of fifty or thereabouts — who, I
found, was regarding me with considerable
curiosity — by remarking that it was a
beautiful evening.

'If anyone had told me,' he rejoined,
much more to the point, 'a fortnight ago,
Herre, that I should ever drink a pot in your
company, I'd have punched him for trying
to make a fool of me—Michael Michaelis.'

'You thought I was lost?'

'Herre, when I saw you with these eyes—
the eyes of Michael Michaelis—in your nut-
shell of a boat upon the lake and the Föhn
signalled, if I'd thought about it at all—
which I didn't—I might have thought the
lake would throw up your body to be buried
decently in Brunnen churchyard, but not
that I should ever drink a pot in your
company.'

While we talked, I watched the men

quaffing their beer, and watched Thérèse as she flitted hither and thither, waiting on them; her cheeks more warmly coloured than usual; her eyes sometimes smiling approbation, sometimes flashing reproof; her abundant black hair braided into one long plait, falling far below her waist; her trimly fitting scarlet bodice showing to perfection the beauty of her figure; her short full skirt allowing all admiring gazers to see the neat ankle and the pretty arched foot.

And as I gazed, filled with that restless discontent, which attends the second stage of convalescence—when we begin to feel our weakness—I grew indignant and wrathful.

At the other end of the room, opposite the windows, was a sort of bar, behind which stood Fleurette and Peter's Nick. It was there that Thérèse and William took the empty pots to be refilled, and this business was carried on so rapidly for a time that

Thérèse's pretty feet hardly seemed to touch the floor as she ran from one to another.

'*Zwei Hamburger, Fleurette.*'

'*Ein Nürnberger Schnitt* for Michael Michaelis.'

'Thérèschen, *Herze*. Have you got any double Bavarian?'

'Not for you, Peter Kunze.'

'And why not for me, *Mädel*, if I've got the money to pay for it?'

Thérèse only looked at him. Everyone else stopped drinking and looked too.

Peter shuffled uneasily upon his seat, muttering that he was *Herr* in his own house, and wasn't going to have the law laid down to him by other folks' *Mädel*. But Thérèse stood steady, and I saw Peter's Nick roll his shirtsleeves a trifle higher and stand at attention.

'And there's more than one *Schenke* and more than one pretty girl in Brunnen,' he added.

Thérèse never moved, but Peter's Nick gave his shirt-sleeve another roll, and drew a step nearer.

' *Schäme dich, Peter Kunze!* '

The words were scarcely audible, and yet it seemed as if the breath to utter them had gone forth from every mouth present. Peter dashed down his pot and went away in a rage.

' Why wouldn't she give it him? ' I said.

' Double Bavarian costs double price,' answered Michael Michaelis laconically, ' and Peter's got a sick wife.'

' He will go elsewhere.'

' *Ja wohl,* he will go elsewhere.'

' And can the host afford to lose his customers like that? '

Michael looked at me with mild surprise in his mild eyes.

. ' He will come back to-morrow, Herre. It doesn't answer here in Brunnen to quarrel with Thérèse.'

'Why not?'

'Ah, why not, Herre? It would take more than is in me to answer that. She isn't like any other *Mädel*, isn't Thérèse.'

I began to grow still more restless and discontented. It angered me to see those dimpled shoulders so close to the rough coats of the lads, to notice how smilingly she heard the endearing epithets by which she was continually addressed. It infuriated me to see her exposed to the gaze of so many masculine eyes, and to feel that her grace and loveliness were made use of for a marketable purpose. Could any girl, specially could Thérèse, with that inflammable French blood coursing through her delicate veins, remain unsullied in such an atmosphere? But the worst was to come.

There were three tables in the room. Two were crowded by aborigines, one was occupied —sparsely now, for the season was drawing

to its close—by strangers. There were two
Italians, two Frenchmen, two or three Germans. All were talking rapidly; the Frenchmen in a low aside.

Riding rampant upon that gaunt hobby
horse of Old England—Strict Propriety—I
angrily pushed back my chair, inwardly resolving to take the first opportunity to remon-
strate with William as to the life his daughter
was leading. Some vague notion of a respectable English boarding-school where I
could pay a deep debt of gratitude, and cause
a hedgeside rose to be trained into a fit standard for an English parterre, rose into my
mind, when certain words falling on my ear
sent me headlong from Strict Propriety into
the slough of unmistakable Bohemianism.

'I have never before seen a girl half so
beautiful!'

The speaker was one of the Frenchmen,
a handsome young fellow of four or five

and twenty, with a refined face, yet sensual eye; and that eye, beaming with no ray of purity, was fixed upon the swelling *Mieder* of Thérèse.

'And what a figure, *sacrement*! Clémence would want to kill her.'

'*Taisez-vous, Brissot*; one is listening.'

'Bah! only an *Anglais*; that makes nothing.'

Whatever it 'made' I meant to hear the rest of the conversation if I could. With my eye negligently turned towards the table, round which the aborigines, their thirst somewhat allayed, were beginning to talk noisily, I listened intently.

'Yesterday I wrote to Clémence that I was coming, but to-day I think I will disappoint her.'

'Ah, I have not known you since we were students together at the Lycée without finding out your weak point, Brissot. Be satisfied with Clémence; she is beautiful enough, is she not?'

'I thought so yesterday, but to-day her image on my retina looks faded and insipid.'

'Faithless gallant! but have a care! One has told me that this girl is as virtuous as she is beautiful.'

'They told me that of Clémence.'

'That means you don't believe it.'

'That means, *mon ami*, exactly what you please to interpret it.'

'Brissot, I am not going to help you.'

'*Mon cher*, I shall do very well without your assistance.'

If there had been any blood in my body to boil, it would have boiled now, I am sure. Full of wrath, I watched Thérèse and the dark eye following her. Full of wrath, I vowed to do my utmost to take her away from such a life.

In the meantime the aborigines began to

rise from their seats, and I concluded that the evening was over.   But no ; Peter's Nick and William, assisted by a few volunteers, were clearing the room for a dance.   And the door opening, in came, blushing and giggling, a number of blooming daughters of the soil, evidently delighted at the noble display of partners awaiting them.   The strangers rose too, smiling, quite willing to join in the amusement.

Someone—I think it was Peter's Nick— lifted me into a corner, where I could look on, the only spectator.

CHAPTER XVIII.

A BLOW FOR A KISS.

Saw a boy a rosebud sweet,
Rosebud in the thicket,
And a green stem was its seat;
Quick he ran with eager feet,
All in haste to pick it.
Rosebud, rosebud, rosebud red,
Rosebud in the thicket.

Broke the stem whereon it grew,
Pulled it from the thicket;
Rosebud said, The deed shalt rue,
I've a thorn that's keen and true,
Through thy hand I'll prick it.
Rosebud, rosebud, rosebud red,
Rosebud in the thicket.

Translated from GOETHE (*Lieder*).

'MONSIEUR did not know it was my *Namenstag.*' It was Thérèse's sweet voice which just murmured these words at my ear.

'No I did not know it.'

'Monsieur looks grave and tired. If I did not just now feel too good-humoured to say anything unkind, I would say, cross. But perhaps monsieur is thinking of the beautiful lady?'

'No, Thérèse; I was thinking of you.'

'Oh, I don't feel honoured. For monsieur's brow is clouded, his eye angry, his lip morose. And not a word of congratulation for my *Namenstag*!'

'You expect me to congratulate you for having grown—how old is it?—among these men. Just now I feel more inclined to *warn* you—to tell you——'

'Warn me—tell me—what do you mean, monsieur? If I had not nerves of iron I might be frightened to death. But out with your warnings; they won't improve with keeping, any more than beer does when the bottle is opened.'

'Well, are you going to dance?'

'To dance, I? Ask the sun if it is going to shine, or the water to ripple, or the bird to sing. Really, monsieur, you are preposterous. You'd better go back to bed again.'

'I can't prevent you, of course. I have no authority over you. If I had,' I added savagely, 'I would not let a single man here put his arm round your waist, I would not let a soul in the room call you by those caressing names. But—you seem to like it.'

'Monsieur, you are detestable, you are odious, you are wicked. As if the poor lads meant any harm! It is you who are full of bad thoughts, or you would not imagine evil where there is none.'

We were both now in a fury. Thérèse's pale cheek was crimson, her eyes full of indignant tears, her lip bleeding from the cruel curb of the pitiless white teeth.

'If you were able to dance, monsieur —which you are not, Englishmen can do

nothing—I would not dance with you. I
detest you, monsieur. You have hurt me
more than I can bear with your vile innu-
endoes. I will never forgive you, and never
speak to you again.'

'All that, mademoiselle, which only proves
what a temper you have—a temper requiring
the severest discipline—will not prevent my
doing my utmost to prevail with your father
to put a stop to this. You have saved my
life. I am not going to forget what I owe
you.'

'I throw your gratitude back in your
teeth, monsieur,' cried Thérèse, her tears
dried up in the fire of her wrath, and forgetting with true woman's inconsistency her
vow of never speaking to me again. 'You
shall not make a strait-laced English miss
of me. I'll die first. Let me go, monsieur.
How dare you touch me? Are you any better
than another?'

We had quite forgotten caution, both of us, but fortunately our raised voices were drowned in the noise of the arrangements for the dance, and in the welcome given to the new-comers. Now the ladies were being regaled with some hot beverage, which diffused a fragrant odour, and the young men were selecting their partners. There was a universal call for Thérèse. I saw the Frenchman advancing, and I spoke hurriedly:

'Hate me as much as you will, Thérèse, but don't dance with that man.'

'What man, monsieur?'

'That Frenchman coming towards you.'

'That handsome man! And why not, pray?'

'Because I have the strongest reason for wishing that you should not.'

.Her red lip curled scornfully as she answered:

'And that is just why I shall do it.

Besides, he is a Frenchman. Frenchmen know how to dance ; *they* are not stupid.'

'I will call your father.'

'He has been sent for to the village, monsieur ; I saw him leave the room a moment ago. And I shall do as I like.'

The young Frenchman advanced with a low bow, soliciting the honour of her hand for the dance. And with a mocking curtsey to me, she put her hand upon his arm, and was led to her place among the dancers.

The music struck up. Two or three fiddlers had found accommodation behind the bar for that purpose. Even Fleurette was being escorted by Peter's Nick to the bottom of the row, and one or two of the men who had not been fortunate enough to secure lady partners jocosely led out substitutes of their own sex. In a few seconds the room was in a whirl ; quicker and quicker moved the dancers, until girlish cheeks glowed

in emulation of the scarlet bodices, and bodices
themselves rose and fell more rapidly to the
time of the quickened heart-beat. Moppert,
too, had caught the infection, and was whirling a very stout *Dirne*, whose waist the little
man could only half encircle, round with the
others.

I will not enter into further details of the
dance. I only watched Thérèse, transferred
from one pair of masculine arms to another.
My anger waning, left me sick and faint. I
was just making a sign to Peter's Nick to take
me back into my room when a catastrophe
occurred.

I know now from her own innocent con-
fession that Thérèse's fury at my reproof arose
in great measure from her own inward conviction that I was not wholly wrong. The
terms of endearment, suitable enough for her
childhood, were beginning to arouse in her
womanhood a frequent feeling of shame. My

cruel probing instrument had sounded the new wound to the bullet rankling there, and the first rebound at the smart carried her beyond consideration for anything but the intolerable pain.

Of course the Frenchman knew nothing of all this. Her ready and apparently delighted consent to dance with him; her smiling reception of his, at first cautious, and ever bolder and broader, compliments carried him beyond the bounds of prudence. How could he know that her smiles were all subterfuge, her ear deaf to his voice ? As, in the whirl of the dance, her sweet flushed face came into close proximity to his, he pressed his lips to it with a sharp sound, distinctly heard above the moving feet and the strains of the music.

My indignation took away what little strength I had and forced me to keep my invalid chair, the most helpless creature in the room. I saw the smile, trembling on the lips of the maidens, reflected rather ominously in the eyes of their partners. Then everyone stood still, as if the significant sound had broken the spring which set them in motion.

For they knew the maiden better than he did—better than I.

Thérèse had torn herself away from the arms of her partner, and now stood facing him, her cheek as pale as the whitewashed wall of the *Schenkstube*. As for him, he stood feigning the smile of indifference, though he knew now that he had made a terrible mistake. His friend stood anxiously in the background, looking on eagerly.

' *Er wird Feigen kriegen, aber keine süssen,*' said someone standing near me.

The pallor on Thérèse's cheek was giving place to a burning blush, an angry light flashed out of her dimmed eye, and even her dimpled shoulders were so deeply dyed that the *Mieder* seemed to pale beside them. Then the fury rushed into her hand—that restless hand so quick to respond to any summons from the brain.

The next moment another sharp sound resounded through the room. There was an involuntary 'Oh!' from the Frenchman, and a laugh of approval from every other mouth present.

With one hand on his swelling cheek, the mortified Frenchman made good his retreat. I looked round for Thérèse, but she was gone.

There was no more dancing that evening. Peter's Nick and Fleurette tried to break up the whispering groups, who only separated to depart.

Then Peter's Nick carried me to bed, and I saw Thérèse that evening no more.

CHAPTER XIX.

UNSOLVED PROBLEMS.

I cannot tell the reason why
I like her kisses so,
Yet never beg one ; she'd reply,
I sadly fear, with No.
My lips meet hers as doth the bee
Sweet honey sip, instinctively.

Just as the zephyr woos the rose,
I woo ; no 'Lovest me ?'
Falls from my lips, yet her cheek glows
A full response and free.
Ah me ! I never saw the dart,
Till, subtly aimed, it pierced my heart.

Adapted from UHLAND.

IT is undoubtedly true that a good, down-right, hearty quarrel is often more efficacious in cementing friendship into an indissoluble bond than long years of pacific passivity, that the tenderest friendships of our lives are watered by abundant tears, and that true love never does run smooth.

Nevertheless, if quarrelling is essential, it is also very bitter. The storm passes over bowed heads, and the period after the fury of the tempest until the return of the sunshine is one of profound depression.

I passed a very restless night after my first serious quarrel with Thérèse, seeing her ever anew in my dreams with angry averted face, and hearing anew the ominous sound and the dubious laughs succeeding it.

At last the morning dawned and the sun streamed in through my window, but it brought no sunshine into my soul. The higher it rose, the lower sank my spirits. For the more I sought to analyse my own motives for my attack on Thérèse, the more despicable they appeared. I had armed myself with the sword of jealousy and the shield of uncharitableness to do battle with the sunbeam for shining alike on all. If Thérèse would but come, that I might show her how ready I was to forgive.

But she did not come. How could I expect her to come? There are insults too gross to be forgiven. I had been measuring her by the petty conventional standard, beside which she rose as lofty and spotless as her own Alps. I had cast dirt on the hedgeside rose for rejoicing other eyes as well as my own, though I knew well, even when my anger, the baleful blaze of jealousy, was at. its hottest, that no fair English girl, however guarded, was surrounded by thorns more keen and sharp for the punishment of those who would touch as well as admire than this sweetest *Heideröschen*.

So the refrain of my elegy resolved itself into :. Oh, if Thérèse would but come, that I might implore her to forgive me !

Nevertheless she came not.

Only Fleurette came to give me my medicine and the coffee, which this morning tasted bitter as gall; only William, graver than usual, but stubbornly silent as to the cause of his gravity; only Moppert, hovering round my easy chair like a parent bird round a threatened nestling; only evening darkening into night, with a restless wind sobbing outside my window, like a lost spirit, seeking rest and finding none.

Strive to retain Hope when she would fly from you; compel the fickle goddess to yield to your desire; try abduction, if prayers are unavailing; clasp her to your bosom until her struggles cease and she remains motionless— the corpse of a dead Hope, more terrible than aught else on earth! Rather turn your face to the wall and read there the dread message of Despair, which has at least the merit of consistency : 'Mene, Mene, Tekel, Upharsin.'

Again and again I closed my eyes and

tried to forget the hungry, gnawing pain which supplemented the first sharp agony, striving to accept the grisly, philosophic belief that pain exists only in the imagination. I had no power to wrestle with it. It baffled every effort, and, like an insolent conqueror, put its cruel foot upon my neck.

. . . . .

' Monsieur ! '

Just a whisper, the faintest whisper possible, yet shaking every nerve within me like a clap of thunder. I thrust away my dead Hope and hushed my heart's beat to listen.

' Monsieur ! '

It *was* Thérèse's voice, and it was soft and supplicating and ended in a sob. I opened my eyes, and there she stood in real flesh and blood beside me ! The lamp cast its full light upon. her, and I could see how sad she was, her eyes reddened with much weeping, her sweet, pale face down-turned ; profound dejection in the hang of her heavy head : profound submission in her attitude, which, as I gazed, sank to the lowest depth of humiliation. With a fresh burst of tears she flung herself passionately on her knees by my bedside and hid her streaming eyes in the coverlet.

A moment before I had cast away my dead Hope, and now behold her again, all the lovelier after her resurrection ! no longer a pampered mistress, but a trembling wife, caressing the hand which had murdered her. A moment before I had cried 'Peccavi' with the loudest, now I was most unexpectedly raised from the lowly position of a suppliant into the lofty one of a magnanimous absolver.

With a rapid reversion of my mental attitude, I turned a cold shoulder towards lovely Hope—for was she not eclipsed altogether by plump and well-favoured Certainty ?

—and I let Thérèse sob on; so sorry, that my heart ached, and yet so glad that I could have burst out into a peal of triumph.

But it was not in the girl's nature to do anything for long. After a while she raised her head and fixed her dark eyes, still brimful of tears, upon my face. As she opened hers I closed mine and feigned to sleep.

'Monsieur is not sleeping, I know. I saw his eyes wide open just now.'

No answer.

'Monsieur, shall I give you your medicine?'

Still silence.

'Monsieur'—in an agitated and alarmed voice—'will you not speak to me?'

'Certainly, Thérèse, *I* never made a vow not to speak to you again.'

'Monsieur, why do you speak so coldly and cruelly? I *cannot* bear it. Why do you offer me a stone when I ask for bread?'

'Thérèse, yesterday I implored you to take

the bread I offered, and you cast it from you and trampled it under your feet.'

' And was I not punished for it, monsieur ? Were you not a witness to my disgrace ? Did I not break my teeth upon the stone I picked up for myself?'

'I certainly hope it proved unpalatable to you.'

' Unpalatable ! It sickened me, monsieur. It poisoned me. Yesterday I was honoured even by my enemies; to-day I am a byword in Brunnen. And if you hate me too——' Here she broke down into a sob again. (Good heavens! is it from God or the devil that we get the power to hurt those most whom we love most tenderly?)

' I do not hate you, Thérèse. I am only sorry for you ; specially sorry that you cannot distinguish friends from ene-mies.'

' And being sorry for me in that tone,

monsieur, is worse than hating me. It shows that you, too, despise me, as I despise myself.'

I lay quiet, and Thérèse, after a few despairing sobs, grew quiet too. So quiet, that at last, terrified at the idea that she had gone away, I opened my eyes again.

But there was no fear of that. She had risen from her knees, but was still standing beside me, her pale cheek wet with despairing tears, her full lips quivering, her pretty little *retroussé* nose reddened from suppressed emotion. My heart began to relent and to swell up into my throat as I looked upon her, and the whip she had given me all but fell from my hand.

'Monsieur,' she said again, and her voice was very humble and beseeching, 'do let me give you your medicine. I'm sure you have not taken it.'

'And I am sure, Thérèse, that I have.'

'Two full tablespoonfuls three times a day without me there to make you?'

'Yes, Thérèse, even without the stimulus of your presence I have taken them.'

'But your *Suppe*? I know you have eaten nothing all day. I saw Fleurette bring it out untouched, and if I had not been so—so——'

'So perverse and naughty, Thérèse?' I said suggestively, and with difficulty suppressing the laugh—a remorseful laugh though—that was rising.

'No, monsieur,' she said, colouring angrily, 'I was not going to say that; I was going to say, " sorry and ashamed," but now that it pleases you to mock, as well as despise, me, I will not give you the satisfaction of knowing how very, very mis——I mean, how little I care for your anger or approbation, and if it had not been for my duty as your nurse——'

'Ho, ho! mademoiselle,' I thought, 'you

have not had enough, have you? Very well,
I know your raw spot now, thank heaven!'

After those last angry observations from
Thérèse, another long pause succeeded, so
long that as the slow seconds ticked themselves away it seemed never ending. Finally,
however, it was broken by another timid
inquiry.

'Shall I raise the pillow at your he d,
monsieur, before I go, and tuck you in?'

'Thank you, I am quite comfortable.'

'Good night, monsieur.'

'Good night, Thérèse.'

This time she made an angry movement
towards the door, and my heart stood still
with terror. My lips were opening to call
her back, in another minute she would have
been my absolute mistress; when, for the
second time, with marvellous shortsighted-
ness, she put the dropped reins into my
hands.

Turning back, before her fingers had even touched the door-latch, she sank upon her knees again, and clasping her hands imploringly, said, with a fresh burst of tears : 'Monsieur, *cannot* you forgive me ? '

'Certainly, Thérèse, when I am asked.'

'But I *do* ask you, monsieur, I *do*. You force me to drink the cup of humiliation to the dregs, but even it is sweet compared with the nauseous draught I mixed for myself yesterday. Monsieur, say—I ask it on my knees, as I should ask it of the holy Mother of God—say : "Thérèse, I am not angry with you any more. I forgive you from the bottom of my heart."'

'Thérèse, I forgive you.'

' " From the bottom of my heart," monsieur.'

'From the bottom of my heart ; and more, I ask you just as earnestly, just as humbly, to forgive me.'

'You, monsieur?' looking up delighted.

'Yes, I, Thérèse. It was right of me to warn you, but it was infamous, inexcusable, atrocious, to do it as I did.'

'Go on, monsieur. Now that you are drinking with me I find humiliation the sweetest draught imaginable.'

'If you were miserable all day and all night, I was ten times more miserable. If you had not come to me, I must have come to you.'

'What a pity I did not wait, monsieur, though, after all, I think I would rather be at your feet than have you at mine.'

'That is because you are the sweetest, most generous girl in the world.'

'Take care, monsieur. Do not undo what you have done. I feel really *good* to-night and couldn't say a cross word to Fleurette or Peter's Nick, whatever happened. I have been as crusty as a bear to them all

day, but I must make it up somehow. As to
my father, poor dear! he has had a hard
time of it, but to-morrow he will not know
what has come to Thérèse, so velvety will
be the slipper with which I shall rule him.
Don't spoil what has made you a benefactor
to the household, monsieur, for it is spoiling
which has developed in me " a temper requiring the severest discipline." '

'Which is quite true, mademoiselle; yet
you would not be Thérèse without it. Un-
salted meat is tasteless, but there is such a
thing as an overdose.'

'Ah, I understand monsieur very well.
I may be as disagreeable as I please to other
people, only not to monsieur. I may scold
Fleurette and Peter's Nick till I am hoarse,
and monsieur rather relishes it than other-
wise; I have seen him smiling at such times
with anything but acrimony. I may scratch
other people's eyes out, only I must be sure

to sheath my claws in velvet when I touch monsieur. I am not blind to monsieur's faults, *Gott bewahre!* I have my own scales, wherein I weigh him, and the faults are heavy enough, goodness knows, yet——'

'Yet what, Thérèse?' For she stopped suddenly, blushing crimson to her finger-tips; even her eyes seemed to glow as eyes do when inward emotion is at its strongest.

' Yet I will not run the risk of quarrelling with you again to-night,' she continued slowly, almost dreamily, as if her thoughts had fled from her words. 'To-night, monsieur; at least, to-night, we will part friends.'

But all the animation had died out of her face, and over the dear, tender, womanly eyes, which were fast filling again, fell a dense shadow. I saw her slight frame seized with a sudden shiver, I saw her cheek paling until it was almost of the ghastly hue of death.

'Good-night, monsieur,' she said solemnly.
'*Leben Sie wohl.*'

'Say "Adieu," Thérèse. I don't like
"*Leben Sie wohl*;" it sounds—well, it sounds
too much like a final parting, and we shall
meet again to-morrow.'

'We shall meet again to-morrow,' she repeated, yet her sweet voice was toneless and
constrained. 'I will say "Adieu" if you like
it better, monsieur; and what *can* be better
than to commend you to God?'

'Let us shake hands, Thérèse.'

'Is that shaking hands, monsieur?' for I
had imperatively drawn her sweet face very
close to mine, in spite of her resistance. 'Fie,
monsieur, how do you dare to kiss, when
you find it so wrong of others even to touch
me?'

'Because we have quarrelled and are
making it up, Thérèse. Now it is your turn.'

In the midst of the almost fierce negation

to my request which was agitating her lips she suddenly changed her mind, wrenched herself free from my clinging hands, and unconstrained, stooped low over me, leaving a warm kiss, and its twin-sister, a warm tear, upon my cheek. Then she was gone, her parting legacy the indelible impression of her soft lips upon my face, and in my brain many conflicting thoughts and wishes which *would* not assimilate.

Among others, whether the exquisite pleasure which her kiss had given me was not an emotion totally inconsistent with my love for the unknown goddess.

Whether I could ever say again with a shadow of truth that my heart, beating violently under my hand, had not been agitated by this second embrace.

Whether I should be able to look Moppert in the face again.

Whether it would not be desirable to

begin my crusade to the rescue as speedily as possible, or—abandon it.

Whether any man before me had ever been in love with two women at the same time, or whether I was a horrible *lusus naturæ* among my species.

Whether, finally, I should sleep for the night, and if so, whether my dreams would be haunted by the imploring face of La Blonde or the tear-stained one of La Brune.

Whether, post—finally, I wasn't a fickle monster who deserved neither.

CHAPTER XX.

PROSIT !

I laugh at every highly learned ox,
Who puffs himself as model for my mind ;
I laugh at all the cowards, fools and blind,
Who threaten me with weapons orthodox.
For when the seven blessings that were given,
Are crushed between Fate's cruel hands, and after,
Thrown down in cold contempt before our feet ;
And when within us even our heart's beat
Is hushed—our soul 's with pain and anguish riven,—
What have we left but wild and cynic laughter ?

HEINE.

It was with no discomposure that I heard, when I awoke the next morning after a night of sound and refreshing sleep, the rain drops pattering thick and heavy against my window-panes. For within my heart all was serenity and sunshine, the remembrance of the pain I had suffered only served to enhance the profound sense of ease and peace which now possessed me, the storm which had threatened to wreck my friendship with Thérèse was but an animating reminiscence, now that that friendship was anchored upon a rock.

So, as a hand was laid upon the door-latch after the preliminary rap and the customary ' *Herein*,' I turned my face away, smiling in anticipation of the pleasure awaiting me, yet wilfully postponing it; partly to gratify the feeling, which, oddly enough, often prompts us to show most indifference where we feel least, partly to make her—the darling!—as eager as I was.

But there was no half-imperative, half-beseeching ' Monsieur,' though my ears were wide open to be charmed by it. And the heavy footfall approaching my bed was surely not that of Thérèse. However wickedly inclined to tease me the maiden might be, she

could never have imitated Fleurette to *that*
perfection. But, hoping against hope, I would
not look up yet.

'Herre!' It *was* Fleurette (oh! cruel,
cruel Thérèse!)

'Herre, will you have your coffee? It is
late.'

Never had Fleurette's stolid, unimpression-
able, sallow, large-featured and high cheek-
boned face appeared to me so odious before.
First wishing her and the coffee—well, never
mind where, I inquired impatiently:

'Where is the Fräulein?'

'Eh? I am a little deaf in one ear.'

I shouted my question anew into the hand
with which she made a trumpet for the other.

'*Das Fräulein?* Ah! der Herr may well
ask where *she* is. But the master may thank
himself for it. He wouldn't heed what I told
him when she was little, and now she's got the
upper hand, got the power without the sense.

I knew how it would be, years ago, and more's the pity that he didn't heed me.'

' Where is she ? '

'Gone down to Brunnen, sir, in the pouring rain, to see an old woman there who is ill. That's what she told the master. But if *he* chooses to believe it, *I* don't. Why, Madame Sauerwein was just as ill yesterday, and there was no talk of going to see her then, though the sun shone. It's the rheumatism, which doesn't come nor go in an hour. When a maiden like Thérèse is as crazy as that to have her own way, anybody with sense in their heads may know that there's another reason besides the one she gives. *Irgend ein Mannsperson, wahrscheinlich.* But it's none of my business.'

I thought she seemed to make it very much her business, though. I had never ard her speak with so much animation before : her sallow cheek grew warmer in colouring, and her dull, fishy blue eyes brightened to the utmost of their capabilities.

'Shall I bring you your breakfast, Herre?' she inquired again.

I intimated that she might do so, and during her short absence tried to sweeten my bitter disappointment by repeating to myself that Brunnen was close at hand, and that Thérèse would speedily return. I was beginning to find life not only dull, but also insupportable without the maiden; to feel her presence as indispensable to my well-being as a due amount of oxygen in the atmosphere. I could not breathe quite freely in her absence : I was but half alive without her. Only when she was near, smiled or frowned at me, I became my whole self, because she had breathed into me a new breath of life, making me for the first time all that I could be. Yet, though I was supremely conscious of this, I still imagined that my heart was another's.

When I had finished the breakfast which Fleurette brought, I summoned her to come and sit beside me. As Thérèse was not there to be talked to, I would at least talk about her.

The woman came, the inevitable stocking in her hand.

'I suppose you have known Thérèse,' I began, ' ever since she was a baby?'

'Yes, Herre. I came to take care of the. house and the *Kindli* when the *Frau* died.'

'You knew her mother, too, then?'

'As much as ever I wanted to. She was a giddy thing whom folk thought well off to have caught an honest man. There was talk enough about her at one time. And her daughter is as like her as one poppy's like another in the corn.'

The stocking progressed rapidly after this little outbreak of spite, whirling round and round in the hands that held it, like a thing in agony. The expressionless face was capable of one expression when roused. Something deep hidden in the heart had risen to the surface and was looking at me out of the eyes of the speaker. 'Go on, Fleurette,' I murmured. 'Save me, if you can.'

'But what's the use of talking to the men,' she continued; 'put a mountain of common sense on one side and a pretty face on the other, and which among them turns to the mountain? Though it's none of my business.'

'You were never married, I suppose?' I inquired rather maliciously, attributing this last remark to an injured sense of non-appreciation.

'Yes, I was, Herre, and left a widow with three hungry mouths to fill as well as my own. I was but nineteen years old when the Joachim came a-courting me, putting it into my silly head that I should be better off with *him* for a master than the one I'd got.'

'You were not happy in your married life?'

'Happy, Herre? Who is happy? 'Tis but a change of masters for us women, and the master who pays wage is sure to treat us better than the master who doesn't. The men are all alike. Not that it makes any difference to me.'

The rain poured heavily, in a steady, depressing, hopeless kind of way. There was not a single break in the leaden covering of the sky, nor a gleam of brightness anywhere. What did William mean by letting his daughter go out in such weather? What did Thérèse mean by staying away so long? I would reproach her with severity when she returned. I would hide my delight under a show of anger. Would she be submissive or rebellious — shamefaced or indignant? No matter how, if she only came.

For, oh me! longing was passing into pain, and appetite becoming hunger.

'Will she be back soon?' I said, unable further to curb my impatience.

'Soon? Nay, I cannot tell. That'll be as the whim takes her. She never does what you expect her to do. The master has himself to thank for it. Maybe she'll never come back.'

'Woman, what do you mean?'

'You'll do yourself an injury, Herre, if you put yourself out of the way like that. But the men are all alike, every *Hanswurst* among them.'

'What do you mean, I say?'

'Mean? Why, that Peter's Nick, who is as big a fool as ever drew the breath of life, is glowering out on the rain just like you, with a face sour enough to turn the milk. "If you want to be pitched into," I said, "I can do that as well as the *Mädel*.

Flesh and blood wouldn't stand the way she treats you," I said, "let alone bones and sinew. But that's the way of the men, they'd rather have a slap in the face from her than a kiss from another." '

I threw open the casement and let the rain fall upon my heated head. The wind, rushing in cold and wet, seemed to freeze me to my marrow. I shivered and trembled, as it drearily repeated the words of Fleurette : ' Maybe she'll never come back.'

' You'll catch your death, Herre,' said Fleurette, advancing to shut the window. ' Ugh ! how the wind whistles ! You'd think 'twas speaking to you, many a time.'

' What was that ? ' I cried, for the door creaked loudly and the latch trembled as if a spectral hand were laid upon it.

' It's the rain-wind,' answered Fleurette, reseating herself; ' it was like this the first night I took the *Kindli* to my breast along

with my own Lise, who is just of her age.
And the *Frau*, her mother, was lying laid
out in the next room, covered with flowers,
and quiet enough then. I had the laying of
her out myself, and a beautiful corpse she
did make, to be sure. The *Mädel* would make
a beautiful corpse too; I've often thought so.'

As she spoke, the tortured wind broke
out into a prolonged and ominous wail, while
the old worm-eaten *Schenke* trembled to its
basis. The excitement of deferred hope, and
the woman's heartless talk, and the tempest
together, sent the blood whirling into my
temples until they almost burst. I began
to pace the room like a furious caged
animal.

'They were brought up together,' continued Fleurette, folding up her stocking.
'Thérèse and my own *Mädel*, and brought
up just the same except that the one got a
sight of beating and the other got none. And·

my Lise's a good, honest, hard-working girl now, earning her eighty francs a year in Lucerne, though the lads won't have aught to do with her, because of a squint she was born with and a lame leg that no beating would cure. As for the other, if you want to look for her, Herre, go to the *Mannsleut'*—they'll be the ones that can tell you. When she was but a baby she was always in the *Schenkstube* with the lads, and they making as much of her as if she were a countess. But it's none of my business, even if it were any good talking to the men! Better keep one's breath for one's porridge.'

She stumped heavily away, shaking every article in the room during her progress to the door, and leaving me again to my own reflections or to guesses as to what the wind was saying.

It was saying something now to which I was forced to listen, though I would fain have turned a deaf ear to it—something about cruel ingratitude to a benefactor—something about a father wronged and a daughter betrayed—something about a kiss heavily purchased.

A kiss! her kiss! With another wild rush of the wind Comprehension came and looked down upon me, forcing me to understand. I knew now what the wind was saying, and why Thérèse was gone. I knew now what her kiss signified.

Her kiss! Again it burned on my cheek, and now like a criminal brand which could never be effaced—a brand that would stand for ever between me and married happiness.

Marriage? How dared I contemplate marriage, when all sophistical argument was hushed within me for ever; when I was looking upon unveiled Truth and the whip of scorpions she held for my chastisement, and shuddering with dread and unutterable terror at the punishment I was called upon to endure?

For to witness the pain of those to whom we owe much, and whom we have injured, is the most awful punishment God can lay upon us. And oh, how terrible is His wrath! Who may stand when He is angry?

For I knew now that with every fibre of my heart I loved this village maiden—loved her in despite of unknown goddesses, and fidelity, and common sense, and all the rest of it. I knew, too—and the knowledge was a sharp sword dividing the joints and marrow —that she loved me. Oh joy, unutterably divine! pain unendurable! for my dastardly base-born pride was still stronger than my love, and in the fierce conflict which would ensue between them, one—the weaker one— must perish.

I knew now that my love for the beautiful Unknown had been but a phantom of my own creation; but *this* was a flesh-and-blood love, with a beating heart and throbbing pulse, which would bleed if I murdered it. Yet there was no alternative. I must murder it.

And now it came and stood beside me, looking into my eyes with its reproachful ones, and I knew that those tender orbs would haunt me for ever. Love stood alone, un- armed, defenceless, but Pride had an army in its rear. See them rallying behind it, my father, my mother, Lord George Graceless, and Sir Harry Goitt, the world, and the world's wife. Hear them applauding Pride's vehe- mently hissed : ' Impossible ! Though thou art fit to die for love of her, thou canst never make Thérèse thy wife.'

' I might have consented,' so my father seemed to say, ' to a union with the beautiful and accomplished lady, the companion of a Princess, but to this—never. The girl is a *Schenkmädchen*, the *Herzchen* and *Liebchen* of village lads. Worse even than this, she is the daughter of a footman and a lady's-maid.

She belongs to the lowest of the people. A gentleman may ruin any number of the class he likes, but to marry one of them is a crime against society so atrocious that it must be punished, for the protection of society, by social death. Good gracious! if we allowed any such intrusion into our phalanxed ranks, what would become of *Us?* For we cannot but see that in beauty, talent, virtue, these outsiders often—oh, very often!—carry off the palm.'

To these remarks everyone but Love clapped approval. Love stood silent, looking at me.

Fierce and long was the conflict, for, as Moppert said, ' Love is very powerful,' but at last it ceased. They locked my heart up in a dark dungeon, where it would never more be gladdened by the sunshine, and Love lay prostrate and motionless at my feet. I turned my head away, for I feared its breaking eyes.

It was dead; but even in death was stronger than any living thing.

And this, I thought, smiling bitterly, is the happiness which society gives, in exchange for what she has robbed me! It is a curious-looking creature, and contact with it chills me to the marrow of my bones. But Mrs. Grundy has weighed in the balance and declared it not wanting. Prosit to it, therefore! I drink your health, fair (no, not fair—foul—what are words?)—foul creature. Long life to you! What are words? Evidently nothing. Evidently the devil's own invention to mislead us. I am moved to laugh over fools that believe in them. You tell me this is happiness, and I know it is profoundest misery, yet I say 'Amen' to your words. Prosit to it, therefore; prosit, prosit!

I have been sitting for a long time, motion-less and numbed, pondering, half-dead and half-alive, over the enigma of life. I have resolved that death is its only solution.   I am becoming feverishly anxious for that solution. I wonder whether society would approve of the haven towards which I am steering.

Oh, how my aching head burns, and how high my pulse beats against the finger pressing it ; but hurrah, hurrah ! society approves of me !   How cold and benumbed is my im-prisoned heart, but Mrs. Grundy wishes it long life in its dungeon !   How profound is the death of all that made life valuable, but they were offered up to a great Juggernaut ! How I laughed, to be sure, with the German student's gay words of greeting upon my lips. Prosit to you, dearly beloved friends, who have demanded from me more than my heart's blood, and have got it ! Prosit, prosit, prosit !

Then I went to bed and slept, and in the dead of night ' a spirit passed before my face and the hair of my flesh stood up.'

Oh, my murdered love !   Society cannot

exorcise thy spirit, or command thee not to haunt me. Even in my sleep I heard thee turn in thy coffin, and ' an image was before mine eyes, saying——'

Oh, my murdered love! I will not betray thee. Thy words are hidden in my heart, and it is only thou who hast the key thereof.

CHAPTER XXI.

'DOWN TO PENZANCE.'

> Gladly,
> Yet sadly,
> One presence to flee ;
> Ever
> And never
> A pris'ner to be ;
> Now up in heaven,
> Now sad unto death ;
> Love is life's leaven,
> Elixir and breath.
>
> *Translated from* GOETHE.

STRENGTHENED to the resolution by a deep draught of a cordial with which I supplemented my coffee, I determined to tear myself away from temptation, and leave Gütsch as speedily as possible. And as I dressed with trembling hands I tried to persuade myself that I was suffering in a righteous cause. For the iron chains forged by education are the strongest earth knows of, and to rend one's-self free from them the work of a Hercules.

Yet, so inconsistent are we, that, though I resolved never to see Thérèse again, the thought that maybe she had resolved the same maddened me. My pride rose haughtily and defiantly against coercion. If I could not be the high priest of my own sacrifice, I would not submit to it at all.

My toilet completed and the time for action come, the power to act seemed taken from me. My fierce resolve, my fiercer opposition, were subdued into a piteous cry for mercy. ' Let me see her once more,' I cried, 'only once, to say farewell for ever ! '

I sank back into my seat again, my resolution forgotten, every sense turned inward. I sat there for weeks, days, hours—I know not how long. They brought me food and drink, and I ate, I think. They talked to me, and I answered, I think. The body did its best to hide that it was tenantless, that the soul had gone from it.

But I know it was evening, and the heavy sky lightened and the stars shining, when William came and sat down beside me, looking at me with eyes in which was a whole world of pain, but not one gleam of anger.

Then the soul came back into my body with a rush, and the veil which had fallen over my brain was lifted.

' You know all ? ' I said.

' Yes, sir, yes ; I think I do.'

' And you are not angry ? '

' Sir, I will not tell you a lie.   I was that angry with you all yesterday that I could have killed you.   I came to drive you out, and if you had resisted I would have killed you as I would kill a wolf who had crept into the fold.'

He stopped, trembling ; the veins in his bronzed forehead swelling to thick cords, and the sweat covering him like beads.

'I would have killed you,' he continued hoarsely, ' as I would kill an animal whom I had warmed and fed, and who repaid me by mortally wounding that which was dearer to me than my life.'

He covered his face with his strong hands, and I knew, by the quivering of his whole body, that he was weeping. I had sinned, I had sinned, but Heaven knows how heavy then was my punishment!

I put my hand upon his arm; but for the moment it was more than he could bear, and he shook it off fiercely. Then with a painful effort he regained his self-control.

'Sir, I can't shake hands with you yet, I can't. Though I know by what I saw when I came to drive you out; hoping, yes, hoping, that you would resist, and I might have a pretext to kill you—I saw, I say, that you were suffering too, and that stayed me. And now I have promised her, my maiden, and you

wouldn't be safer with the mother who bore
you than you are with me. You wouldn't, I
say, you wouldn't.'

He spoke loudly, as if trying to convince
someone who was stoutly incredulous, and he
clenched his hands with the passionate vehemence of a man who *must* hurt somebody,
even if it be only himself.

'And I am glad you are not drowned, I
am glad; but oh, if it had pleased God A'mighty
to let someone else draw you out of the lake!'

'William,' I cried, 'my sin has been great,
but you think worse of me than I deserve. I
am afraid you think——'

'I think my maiden's heart is broke, sir,
that's what I think. If I thought worse than
that, no power on earth should save you—no,
nor no power in heaven neither.'

'Have you sent her away?' The question was forced from my lips. I could not
keep it back any longer.

For my heart began to heave and chafe in
its dungeon, and my lips to tremble with passionate yearning to taste once more what I
had forsworn for ever.   I had resolved to
give my maiden up, but like the drunkard
who has resolved never to touch another drop
of that which has unmanned him, like the
opium-eater who, knowing what he must pay
for his ecstasy, has resolved to touch the
poison no more, I trembled from head to foot
with the vehemence of my desire.   Resolution,
unable to cope with Passion, fell prostrate.   I
must see her again or I should die.

'Yes, sir,' answered William, not only to
the question, but to the unspoken thought, 'I
have sent her away.   You must never see her
again.'

'It's been bore in upon me,' he continued,
'to speak to you clear and open, and to save
others if I can from that which she has
suffered.   For young gentlemen like you,

brought up to think the world was made for
'em, do a sight o' wickedness, and cause such
misery all along o' thoughtlessness, as might
make the angels in heaven weep to think on;
but so far as we are concerned it might ha'
been worse. My maiden's heart is broke, but
there is no stain upon her honour.'

'I never had a thought concerning her
that was not as pure as herself,' I interrupted.

' Ah, sir,' said William, ' deeds is like words;
they spring up we hardly knows how, and are
awful, unalterable facts before we had quite
shaped 'em into thoughts. The road to sin is
like the road down our glaciers—soft and
smooth and easy. We slide down, down,
faster and faster, and there we are over the
precipice, lost for ever, before we had even
seen to what we were driving.'

I hung my head, and William went on:

'There's a deal in bringin' up, sir, and
maybe if I'd been brought up as badly as you

I might ha' been no better. But, thank God,
I wasn't. Sin was made hard to me, sir. I'll
tell you just a little story out o' my life, and
let it be a warning to you.

'I were born in Cornwall, down to Penzance
—maybe you've heard tell o' Penzance—and
my mother were a Wesleyan. I used to go
with her to Gwennap Pit to hear Wesley
preach, and I never forgot it. We lived in a
almshouse, for my father were dead—he died
before I can remember.

'There was a old Quaker gentleman who
lived near Penzance, and my mother had been
a servant in his fam'ly—'twas he who got her
into the almshouse, where we was very comfortable. He lived in a curious old house ; it
had been a cottage and had got added to, here
a room and there a room, as they was wanted.
This house stood in the most beautiful garden
you can imagine. I've seen heaps of gardens,
but never one like that ; and as for flowers

and fruit, there never was any like them in that garden down to Penzance.

'Well, I used to do a day's weeding now and then in this garden, and one day I was working there, and the strawberries was ripe and the day was very hot, and as I worked the smell of 'em came towards me so sweet and temptin', and I couldn't help thinkin' about 'em.

'Now I had been brought up honest. My mother used to say 'twas all one whether you stole a pin or a sovereign, and I never before thought o' tastin' unless some was given to me. But it was hot and I was dry, and my eyes kept wanderin' to the strawberries and to one in particklar. There was such heaps on 'em.

'"Thou shalt not steal," something seemed to say in my ear.

'But I was so dry. Well, I would go and get a drink of water.

'There was two ways to the well. One led

right through the strawberries; the other way was longer round.

'I knew which way I ought to take very well, but somethin' else seemed to say that I was a downright coward; that 'twas a heap braver to go into the thick o' temptation than to run away from it, and I listened to this second voice. I didn't drive it away. I listened to it.

'Oh, sir, that ain't true courage. Them as go in pride of heart to the brink o' temptation have no call to wonder if they fall over.'

He sighed deeply, then went on :

'Well, sir, I hadn't listened long before I acted. I went through the strawberries, and before I had taken a dozen steps my eyes seemed forced to look at 'em, and I saw one— oh, so big and ripe and juicy !—and my hand seemed forced to take. What can you expect? When you listen to the devil, he soon teaches you that he is a heap cleverer than you are.

'So I stooped and picked, and before I knew rightly what I were doing I had one at my mouth.

'Then something occurred for which I have thanked God ever since, though then I thought I'd rather have died than had it happen. Somebody grasped me by the collar, and I looked up into the eyes of the master

'And the strawberry, untasted, fell from my lips.

'I've seen a many kind faces since the old man died, sir, but I never saw a kinder. Folk has told me since that for all he was a simple Quaker gentleman, he was full of knowledge as well as love, and that many people in the great world knew and honoured him. But whatever he did for others, I know this, that he saved me, and that I shall bless him for it as long as I live.

'I think I see him now, in his broad-brimmed Quaker hat and knee-breeches ; he was rayther short and stout, but looked such a true gentleman as I never saw since. You'd ha' trusted him only to look at him, for there wasn't a harsh line in his face, and his grey eyes, with their bushy white eyebrows, were as kind as they were keen. But I'd rayther anyone in the world had found me stealing than him or my mother.

'" Boy," he said, " what art thou doing ? "

'" 'Twas the first one, sir," I stammered.

'" How many apples dost thou think Eve ate before it was sin ? "

' I sobbed aloud as he asked the question.

'" Now I want to make sin so hard to thee that thou wilt never want to try it again," he said. " What had I better do— flog thee myself or take thee home to thy mother ? "

'" Oh, sir," I said, " flog me yourself, but don't tell my mother."

' " I think I must," he said. " I have no right to deceive her, and besides, if she's the Dorothy of old, she'd never think it was properly done unless she did it herself."

' That was so true that I could not say another word. Everybody who knew my mother knew that. She had never struck me in her life, but I knew if I had to be struck she would a heap rayther do it herself, and that she'd be sure to do it thorough.

' So I was marched out through the beautiful garden to my home in the almshouse, where my mother sat knitting. She looked up amazed as our shadows fell over her; then after a few words from my master looked alone at me.

' Sir, I never needed to be told again what stealing only a strawberry meant to her. And my master let go of my collar to take her hand, saying, in a voice that sounded as if tears had got into it, " Dorothy, if I had known I would have kept it from thee."

'I got my flogging, of course, and no light one neither, but 'twas nothing, nothing after that look. When I went back to my work the next day, I had to go and ask my master to forgive me. He lifted up my chin and looked steadily into my eyes.

' "Now, my son," he said, "remember next time thou art tempted that there's a flogging at the end of it."

' " Yes, sir," I answered, " and my mother."

'Well,' continued William, looking hard at me, 'it were bore in upon me that, maybe, 'twere something with you as with me and the strawberry—you didn't know what road you was going on. One kiss 'ud hurt nobody——'

He paused as if a sudden thought had struck him, and looked before him in blank bewilderment. 'But the strawberry,' he muttered, 'what about it? The soft rain and the sunshine didn't ripen it for that. Was it ripened to be thrown away?—it, the sweetest and the ruddiest.'

The great enigma, the terrible enigma which has racked men's brains oft enough, was suggesting itself to him now, and under the pain of it his strong Christian faith trembled and waxed faint. 'What about the strawberry?' he repeated, 'what about it?'

He did not know that he would have puzzled all the sages and divines the world ever heard of by that simple question. He did not know that behind it lay all knowledge; beyond it, nothing but faith.

END OF THE FIRST VOLUME.

Spottiswoode & Co. Printers, New-street Square, London.